BOOKS BY JAMES MERRILL

Poetry

A SCATTERING OF SALTS   1995
SELECTED POEMS 1946–1985   1992
THE INNER ROOM   1988
LATE SETTINGS   1985
FROM THE FIRST NINE: POEMS 1946–1976   1982
THE CHANGING LIGHT AT SANDOVER   1982
SCRIPTS FOR THE PAGEANT   1980
MIRABELL: BOOKS OF NUMBER   1978
DIVINE COMEDIES   1976
BRAVING THE ELEMENTS   1972
THE FIRE SCREEN   1969
NIGHTS AND DAYS   1966
WATER STREET   1962
THE COUNTRY OF A THOUSAND YEARS OF PEACE   1959
(REVISED EDITION 1970)
FIRST POEMS   1951

Fiction

THE (DIBLOS) NOTEBOOK   1965
THE SERAGLIO   1957, 1987

Essays

RECITATIVE   1986

A Memoir

A DIFFERENT PERSON   1993

Selected Poems

1946-1985

James Merrill

Selected Poems

1946-1985

Alfred A. Knopf   *New York*   *2000*

THIS IS A BORZOI BOOK
PUBLISHED BY ALFRED A. KNOPF, INC.

Copyright © 1992 by James Merrill

All rights reserved under international and Pan-American Copyright Conventions. Published in the United States by Alfred A. Knopf, Inc., New York, and simultaneously in Canada by Random House of Canada Limited, Toronto. Distributed by Random House, Inc., New York.

www.randomhouse.com/knopf/poetry/

The poems included in this collection originally appeared in the following:

First Poems, copyright © 1950 by Alfred A. Knopf, Inc.; copyright renewed 1978 by James Merrill, published by Alfred A. Knopf, Inc.

The Country of a Thousand Years of Peace, copyright 1951, 1952, 1953, 1954, © 1957, 1958, 1970 by James Merrill; copyright renewed 1979, 1980, 1981, 1982 by James Merrill, originally published by Alfred A. Knopf, Inc., revised edition published by Atheneum.

Water Street, copyright © 1960, 1961, 1962 by James Merrill, published by Atheneum.

Nights and Days, copyright © 1960, 1961, 1962, 1963, 1964, 1965, 1966 by James Merrill, published by Atheneum.

The Fire Screen, copyright © 1964, 1966, 1967, 1968, 1969 by James Merrill, published by Atheneum.

Braving the Elements, copyright © 1969, 1970, 1971, 1972 by James Merrill, published by Atheneum.

Divine Comedies, copyright © 1976 by James Merrill, published by Atheneum.

Late Settings, copyright © 1985 by James Merrill, published by Atheneum.

Library of Congress Cataloging-in-Publication Data

Merrill, James Ingram.
   [Selections, 1992]
   Selected poems, 1946–1985 / James Merrill.—1st ed.
   p. cm.
   ISBN 0-679-74731-1 (paperback)
   I. Title.
PS3525.E6645A6   1992
811'.54—dc20   91-58622
                            CIP

Manufactured in the United States of America
Published September 10, 1994
Reprinted Seven Times
Ninth Printing, April 2000

For DAVID JACKSON

CONTENTS

Contents

Contents

From First Poems (1951)

THE BLACK SWAN

Black on flat water past the jonquil lawns
    Riding, the black swan draws
A private chaos warbling in its wake,
Assuming, like a fourth dimension, splendor
That calls the child with white ideas of swans
    Nearer to that green lake
    Where every paradox means wonder.

Although the black neck arches not unlike
    A question mark on the lake,
The swan outlaws all easy questioning:
A thing in itself, equivocal, foreknown,
Like pain, or women singing as we wake;
    And the swan song it sings
    Is the huge silence of the swan.

Illusion: the black swan knows how to break
    Through expectation, beak
Aimed now at its own breast, now at its image,
And move across our lives, if the lake is life,
And by the gentlest turning of its neck
    Transform, in time, time's damage;
    To less than a black plume, time's grief.

Enchanter: the black swan has learned to enter
    Sorrow's lost secret center
Where, like a May fête, separate tragedies
Are wound in ribbons round the pole to share
A hollowness, a marrow of pure winter
    That does not change but is
    Always brilliant ice and air.

3

The Black Swan

Always the black swan moves on the lake. Always
 The moment comes to gaze
As the tall emblem pivots and rides out
To the opposite side, always. The blond child on
The bank, hands full of difficult marvels, stays
 Now in bliss, now in doubt.
 His lips move: I love the black swan.

THE BLUE EYE

Vivid to the myopic are the blue
Reversals blurred within his looking glass:
Held-to-the-nose bouquet of distances
He tries to keep from breathing, asking why
Those veiled hints of a world so near so far
Have never, on this ideal plane, come clear.

Within its oval shimmer wind and dune,
Sundin and sealight in vague unison.
Cocked to the wingbeat they may yet construe,
The vanes of seeing veer back, forth to sound
An iris-deep epitome, dream bound,
Fluent in the idiom of blue.

Sky is the one true likeness. It cannot
Be plumbed and in the mirror it cannot.
Likeness and essence both, the blank azur
Unmirrored of dry mornings is no whit
More potent than this glancing O—for what
He misses here he'll never know was there.

Flighty particulars that would not meet
His eye, adieu! Let others turn in mute
Wonder to foam-glint and blue beach grape, blue
Heron and mussel-bed: each thing's to him
Precious on principle, as idea, as name.
Henceforth it is his pride no sooner to

Frame in a sense the blood-and-thunder Sea
(Its egg acrawl with noon deflecting summary)
Than flash! horizons made of yes and no
Tilt him beyond all telling—empty shell,
Dropped feather, footprint drained of sky. How shall
We know him, then? By the light in his blue eye.

THE BROKEN BOWL

To say it once held daisies and bluebells
    Ignores, if nothing else,
Much diehard brilliance where, crashed to the floor,
The wide bowl lies that seemed to cup the sun,
Its green leaves wilted, its loyal blaze undone,
All spilt, its glass integrity no more.
    From piece to shattered piece
A fledgling rainbow struggles for release.

Did also the heart shatter when it slipped?
    Shards flash, becoming script,
Imperfection's opal signature
Whose rays in disarray hallucinate
At dusk so glittering a network that
The plight of reason, ever shakier,
    Is broadcast through the room
Which rocks in sympathy, a pendulum.

No lucid, self-containing artifice
    At last, but fire, ice,
A world in jeopardy. What lets the bowl
Nonetheless triumph by inconsequence
And wrestle harmony from dissonance
And with the fragments build another, whole,
    Inside us, which we feel
Can never break, or grow less bountiful?

Love does that. Spectral through the fallen dark,
    Eye-beam and ingle-spark
Refract our ruin into this new space,
Timeless and concentric, a spotlight
To whose elate arena we allot
Love's facets reassembling face by face,
    Love's warbler among leaves,
Love's monuments, or tombstones, on our lives.

RIVER POEM

This old man had lavender skin, a handkerchief
Toppling from his breastpocket like an iris.
We on the riverbank watched the gracing rowers
Leaving the shore and watched him watch them leave,
And Charles said: I wonder if they mean to him
As much as I can imagine they mean to him.

Charles was like that. But as evening became
A purple element we stayed there wondering
About the old man—talking of other things,
For although the old man by the time we all went home
Was gone, he kept in view, meandering
As with the current, thinking of rivery things

(We supposed) well into the twilight. We would never
Know, this we knew, how much it had meant to him—
Oars, violet water, laughter on the stream.
Though we knew, Charles said, just how much *he* meant to the
     river.
For he finally left us alone, the strange old man,
But the river stayed at our side, and shone, and ran.

VARIATIONS: THE AIR IS SWEETEST
THAT A THISTLE GUARDS

1

The air is sweetest that a thistle guards
And purple thistles in our blue air burn
And spiny leaves hold close the light we share.
The loose tides sprawl and turn and overturn
(Distant pearl-eaters gorging) on the shore,
While taut between those waters and these words,
Our air, our morning, the poignant thistles weave
Nets that bind back, garland the hungering wave.

2

Midsummer spreads the ticklish mullein leaf,
Rambler and brambles, and his ankles bleed
Who wanders less than gingerly among them;
In winter, holly; later, the bittersweet rose;
Leaves harsh and somber, nettles in November.

Burr, cactus, yucca, the moral thorn that only
A snail can master; plants that bring to mind
Porcupines (bad for dogs), sea-urchins, scorpions:
Near by what silkiest blows a sharp thing grows
And this is good for lovers to remember.

3

Flowers are people
Enchanted by witches—
This we were able
To learn in the nursery,
But thought, being mercenary,
How witches brought candy,
Were easy to hide from
Or frighten with matches.

Listening to Nanny
We laughed till we died
At her warnings, her funny
Despairs, her enticements:
"Be good!"—while in basements
We broke eggs on grindstones,
Pulled apart flowers
And tracked snow inside.

Ah, people are flowers.
They fall helter-skelter
In their first witching weather
Or turn wry like thistles
Who, bristling together,
Brag of their shelters,
Insist that each latest
Is safest, is sweetest.

4

When at midnight Jane took off her mask, the red-
Checkered-lavender and bordered with seed pearls,
She kissed Giovanni as though she had never had
Another lover. Girls
Simpered, yet this was beautiful. Outside,
Veranda lanterns, then darkness and wavegleam
Could make a dry heart seem
To ripple like a warm incoming tide.

Not now the answer, for of course there were
No helpful answers, but the air of questioning
Is what one would remember, would let ring clear
Through chambers echoing
Pain's little plash. Beyond the coral reef
Shot through by cruel, vivid lives, down, down,
Sand settled on a crown,
A lost shape no less there in faint relief.

Just as beneath her mask was Jane. One thought,
Seeing it drop, raked by her sweet, proud smile,
"Beauty so poignant, so intemperate,
Breaks, at a glance, the jail
We damn it to." Remembering love but fearing
The memory of the beloved, I once cut
Three thistles which I put
In a glass of water, then sat beside them, staring,

Asking the flowers, silver under water,
To tell me about time and love and doom,
Those great blue grottos of feeling where the rank intruder
Is moved to think in rhyme.
But the thistles could indicate only that face which came
Abruptly to mock with its usual sated languor
My nakedness, my hunger,
And the thistles took my hand when I reached for them.

5
Three days I wept in the snow, feet bare,
Then to Canossa waved goodbye.
Absolution was a luxury
Only the pure in heart could snare.
I went where the pearl-eaters were.

The air was dazzling in my eye
Accustomed to the mountainous shade
So lately left behind. This showed
I was still short of purity
But it would come assuredly.

Pearl-eaters glimpsed me from afar
Stumbling down the parched foothill.
Forth glittered one on wingèd heel
With napkin dipped in vinegar
Who bade me taste their "humble fare".

In a chair of pearl I sat while gulls
Croaked Cheer! and ate the priceless food.
There was always more, my hostess said.
It bit the tongue like sleeping pills—
Was purity the pace that kills?

So with the pearl-eaters I stayed
Till memory drove me back inland
Where, to my wonderment, I found
Whatever I tasted wherever I strayed
Became at once of pure pearl made.

6
Friday. Clear. Cool. This is your day. Stendhal
At breakfast-time. The metaphors of love.
Lucky perhaps, big Beyle, for whom love was
So frankly the highest good, to be garlanded
Accordingly, without oblivion, without cure.
His heedful botany: not love, great pearl
That forms about a small unlovely need;
Nor love whose fingers tie the birthday bow
Upon the sorry present. Love merely as the best
There is, and one would make the best of that
By saying how it grows and in what climates,
By trying to tell the crystals from the branch,
Stretching that wand then toward the sparkling wave.
To say at the end, however we find it, good,
Bad, or indifferent, it helps us, and the air
Is sweetest there. The air is very sweet.

THE PEACOCK

I speak to the unbeautiful of this bird
    Celestially bored,
That on gnarled gray feet under willows trails
Too much of himself, like Proust, a long brocade
Along, not seen but felt; that's never spared,
    Most mortal of his trials,
  Lifting this burden up in pride.

The outspread tail is drab seen from the back
    But it's worthwhile to look
At what strenuous midribs make the plumage stretch.
Then, while it teeters in the light wind, ah
He turns, black, buff, green, gold, that zodiac
    Of—no, not eyes so much
  As idiot mouths repeating: I.

Consider other birds: the murderous swan
    And dodo now undone,
The appalling dove, hens' petulant sisterhood;
And now this profile that no cry alarms,
Tense with idlesse, as though already on
    A terrace in boxwood
  Or graven in a coat of arms;

And in all these, the comic flaw of nature
    No natural hand can suture,
A lessening—whether by want of shape they fail,
Of song, or will to live, or something else.
How comforting to think blest any creature
    So vain, so beautiful!
  But some have known such comfort false.

A beatitude of trees which shall inherit
    Whoever's poor in spirit
Receives the peacock into cumbersome shade.
Some who have perfect beauty do not grieve,
As I, when beauty passes. They've known merit
    In word, emotion, deed:
  Lone angels round each human grave.

TRANSFIGURED BIRD

I

That day the eggshell of appearance split
And weak of its own translucence lay in the dew.
A child fond of natural things discovered it.

Though it was broken it was very blue,
Pearly within, and lit by sun enough
For it to glow, though broken clean in two.

He ran home with it wrapped in a handkerchief
To where he kept his findings. Here, in a nest,
Robins' eggs hollowed by a pin and a puff;

Moths spread like ferns, then ferns and flowers pressed
Like moths on cotton; a bullfrog, once green;
Minerals, and a few smutched feathers, lest

The world be part forgotten if part unseen.
No longer glowing, but blue as the sky that day,
The shell went on the top shelf. What had been

Inside was nimble and hungry and far away,
And had left behind only this envelope
For a child to take home, and for years mislay.

2

As one who watches two days in some hope
A fertile yolk, until there throbs at last
The point of blood beneath his microscope,

Then rises rinsed with the thought of what has passed,
I watched the big yolk of remembrance swallowed
By the throbbing legend there, that broke its fast,

Grew into shape, soon to be hatched and hallowed,
Whether a bugling bird or cockatrice;
And when the wild wings rose, on foot I followed.

And much was legend long days after this.
I mean that much was read and read aright.
Where the bird went gold plumes fell, which were his.

3
Philippa raised her elbows to the light
As though to lean there watching the red deer
Leap through it, blond as her hair unpinned at night

When by her bed she took a comb to her hair
And gave it lessons in simplicity
Till each long lock was docile and severe;

Then turned as if to smile, smiled then at me,
And in the sudden dark stretched with no fear,
For whom the night was a long nubility.

Reynard, Cock Robin, Bruin and Chanticleer,
Dreaming she ruled these clever animals
She had laughed aloud in her sleep when they came near.

Or shown by lamplight "Mother's valuables"—
Fabergé Easter eggs that lady kept
To look at in her moods. The enameled shells

Sprang wide at a touch, and out each marvel stepped.
In one, some great-grandchildren's miniatures
That a Russian prince smiled at before he slept;

Then from a gold yolk with sharp ruby spurs
A little rooster flaps gold wings and crows
—Inside of it a thumbnail engine whirs;

"And this I think has a fox, but one never knows."
Nor did she know, nor would I tell her ever
How close she was to the flood of time that flows,

Or rather flies, a yellow bird, forever
Beyond, stops only if we stop, to trill
In the thicket yonder, loudest to a lover.

Close in the thicket under her windowsill
The bird of prophecy no song decoys
Sang, while she dreamed and I was somewhat still;

Sang, in a dark the color of its voice,
First of the past, the teeming yolk; sang then
Of fables, findings, shelves of fabulous toys,

Its various images in the minds of men;
Of love. At which she woke. The bird in me
Sang on, a panic in my blood, a pain.

Strange how that music made the loved one's beauty,
Most notable for being brief, of such
A power one could have wept for brevity—

Her hair too much like sun, her love too much
Like ignorance, perhaps? I must begin
To tell her of this music in my touch:

Of God who like a little boy with a pin
Shall prick a hole in either end of the sky
And blow it clean away, the thing within,

Away, before it waste, or hatching fly
Out of his reach in noisy solitude,
Or kill him with the oracle in its eye;

Blow all away, the yolk with its X of blood,
The shelves of jewels away, this drowsing girl
At whose hand, away, the shapely animals fed,

Till the egg is void of all but pearl-on-pearl
Reflections and their blithe meanderings;
Shall, tiring, crush the shell, let the fragments whirl.

4

That day the year, eager to hatch new springs,
Nested in russet feathers by the bare lake.
That day a child who was fond of natural things

Went where light dangled like a bait to take
And found a blue egg which had airily dropped,
A freak of season, down to the hooked brake,

Lifted it out, as children will, but stopped.
He had thought to blow it clean, but there had broken
From the cold shell his chilly fingers cupped

The claw of the dead bird, clutching air, a token
Of how there should be nothing cleanly for years to come,
Nor godly, nor reasons found, nor prayers spoken.

And though it was still early morning he went home
And slept and would not till nearly dusk be woken.

HOURGLASS

Alone, one can but toy with imagery.
I watch this hourglass that has been taught
  Calm flowing such as you teach me,
    For inasmuch as we
Too are sheer crystal and fine red sand brought
From where sun makes a stab at majesty,
With which each thin globe feeds its counterpart,
  This form most holds you to my heart.

For this perhaps a baffled century
Given to grand personifications, feeling
Women had secrets they were not revealing,
    Made it a norm of beauty,
   Called sumptuous figures by its name,
Placed it in rooms where, bland and beautiful
And more genteel than the memorial skull,
   It took their glances, kept them tame,

Kept tame their beauty, but their utterance urged
To a fine effulgence, to a finer trust
That the soul's crystal and the body's dust
  Should never finally be merged.
    Nor would those souls admit
Margins for error which we smile at now
In the transparent teardrop, knowing how,
  Teller of time, time tells on it,

For sand so wears the shift of skintight glass
That, years before it shows, our lives infil-
  trate swifterly the waste none will
   (The waist, I meant) bypass
  As toward his overturn he moves.
Alone I cannot bear this image. You
Are the kind gathering I still falter to.
Love only is replenishment of halves.

WILLOW

If not, why should the willow bend? It bends
High in the air, but to the stream descends
Dipping its as-we-call-them finger-ends

In weedy water, trailing to the touch:
A weeping tree, we say—but with not much
Of willow in the figure, once to such

As we long limbs had lent, though covertly,
Movements more suave, guiding what pangs there be
Into a bearable choreography:

Our hands wrung changes on the mute charade
Of willows: from the simple noises made
By creatures come to drink in the trees' shade

Came sound of women weeping into their hands,
Yielding to hurt's pure flow, depths and demands
The littlest child remembers, understands:

Because of this we never could recall
What we *did* bear, as under water all
Becomes a silvery weightless miracle

In which, presuming on the certitude
Of bodily grace, whatever impulse wooed
Profounder levels rose to air renewed:

Thus, rocked by sorrows, never could we tell
How grave they were, our bodies knowing well
The signs to charm them, alter or dispel:

At times we thought, Gesture is all that grieves:
The hand has slanted (like the willow's leaves)
From touching faces it alone conceives

Willow

Downward to drop its pennies on shut eyes
Before the habit fades of their surprise
Past blood and tissue where remembrance lies.

THE HOUSE

Whose west walls take the sunset like a blow
Will have turned the other cheek by morning, though
The long night falls between, as wise men know,

Wherein the wind, that daily we forgot,
Comes mixed with rain and, while we seek it not,
Appears against our faces to have sought

The contours of a listener in night air,
His profile bent as from pale windows where
Soberly once he learned what houses were.

Those darkening reaches, crimsoned with a dust
No longer earth's, but of the vanishing west,
Can stir a planet nearly dispossessed,

And quicken interest in the avid vein
That dyes a man's heart ruddier far than stain
Of day does finial, cornice and windowpane,

So that whoever strolls on his launched lawn
At dusk, the hour of recompense, alone,
May stumbling on a sunken boundary stone

The loss of deed and structure apprehend.
And we who homeless toward such houses wend
May find we have dwelt elsewhere. Scholar and friend,

After the twelve bright houses that each day
Presume to flatter what we most display,
Night is a cold house, a narrow doorway.

This door to no key opens, those to brass.
Behind it, warning of a deep excess,
The winds are. I have entered, nevertheless,

And seen the wet-faced sleepers the winds take
To heart; have felt their dreadful profits break
Beyond my seeing. At a glance they wake.

From The Country of a
Thousand Years of Peace *(1959)*

THE COUNTRY OF A THOUSAND
YEARS OF PEACE

to Hans Lodeizen (1924–1950)

Here they all come to die,
Fluent therein as in a fourth tongue.
But for a young man not yet of their race
It was a madness you should lie

Blind in one eye, and fed
By the blood of a scrubbed face;
It was a madness to look down
On the toy city where

The glittering neutrality
Of clock and chocolate and lake and cloud
Made every morning somewhat
Less than you could bear;

And makes me cry aloud
At the old masters of disease
Who dangling high above you on a hair
The sword that, never falling, kills

Would coax you still back from that starry land
Under the world, which no one sees
Without a death, its finish and sharp weight
Flashing in his own hand.

THE OCTOPUS

There are many monsters that a glassen surface
Restrains. And none more sinister
Than vision asleep in the eye's tight translucence.
Rarely it seeks now to unloose
Its diamonds. Having divined how drab a prison
The purest mortal tissue is,
Rarely it wakes. Unless, coaxed out by lusters
Extraordinary, like the octopus
From the gloom of its tank half-swimming half-drifting
Toward anything fair, a handkerchief
Or child's face dreaming near the glass, the writher
Advances in a godlike wreath
Of its own wrath. Chilled by such fragile reeling
A hundred blows of a boot-heel
Shall not quell, the dreamer wakes and hungers.
Percussive pulses, drum or gong,
Build in his skull their loud entrancement,
Volutions of a Hindu dance.
His hands move clumsily in the first conventional
Gestures of assent.
He is willing to undergo the volition and fervor
Of many fleshlike arms, observe
These in their holiness of indirection
Destroy, adore, evolve, reject—
Till on glass rigid with his own seizure
At length the sucking jewels freeze.

OLIVE GROVE

The blue wave's slumber and the rocky brow
Almost submerged where while her father slept
Sleep of the blue wave from his forehead leapt
The goddess, dropped her gift, this silvery bough

On him who among olives drowses now
Among these drowsing boughs their trunks express,
Pale paint from tubes so twisted, emptiness
Might sooner have put forth the slumbering green

Than these whose gnarled millennium bestows
(Upon his slumber tentatively marine
For whom endurance, lacking theirs, had been
Too bare an ikon of the mind's repose)

A dream, not of his dreaming, or to wean
Roots from deep earth, rather of how each delves
To taste infusions by whose craft ourselves,
Once dreams in the mind of earth, like olive trees,

Houses, the sleeper and his smile, the quais
And tall sail bent on the blue wave, have grown
Out of that molten center now alone
Uneasy for its melting images.

HOTEL DE L'UNIVERS ET PORTUGAL

The strange bed, whose recurrent dream we are,
Basin, and shutters guarding with their latch
The hour of arrivals, the reputed untouched Square.
Bleakly with ever fewer belongings we watch
And have never, it each time seems, so coldly before

Steeped the infant membrane of our clinging
In a strange city's clear grave acids;
Or thought how like a pledge the iron key-ring
Slid overboard, one weighty calm at Rhodes,
Down to the vats of its eventual rusting.

And letters moulting out of memory, lost
Seasons of the breast of a snowbird . . .
One morning on the pillow shall at last
Lie strands of age, and many a crease converge
Where the ambitious dreaming head has tossed

The world away and turned, and taken dwelling
Within the pillow's dense white dark, has heard
The lovers' speech from cool walls peeling
To the white bed, whose dream they were.
Bare room, forever feeling and annulling,

Bare room, bleak problem set for space,
Fold us ever and over in less identity
Than six walls hold, the oval mirror face
Showing us vacantly how to become only
Bare room, mere air, no hour and no place,

Lodging of chance, and bleak as all beginning.
We had begun perhaps to lack a starlit Square.
But now our very poverties are dissolving,
Are swallowed up, strong powders to ensure
Sleep, by a strange bed in the dark of dreaming.

A RENEWAL

Having used every subterfuge
To shake you, lies, fatigue, or even that of passion,
Now I see no way but a clean break.
I add that I am willing to bear the guilt.

You nod assent. Autumn turns windy, huge,
A clear vase of dry leaves vibrating on and on.
We sit, watching. When I next speak
Love buries itself in me, up to the hilt.

THE CHARIOTEER OF DELPHI

Where are the horses of the sun?

Their masters' green bronze hand, empty of all
But a tangle of reins, seems less to call
His horses back than to wait out their run.

To cool that havoc and restore
The temperance we had loved them for
I have implored him, child, at your behest.

Watch now, the flutings of his dress hang down
From the brave patina of breast.
His gentle eyes glass brown

Neither attend us nor the latest one
Blistered and stammering who comes to cry
Village in flames and river dry,

None to control the chariot
And to call back the killing horses none
Now that their master, eyes ashine, will not.

For watch, his eyes in the still air alone
Look shining and nowhere
Unless indeed into our own

Who are reflected there
Littler than dolls wound up by a child's fear
How tight, their postures only know.

And loosely, watch now, the reins overflow
His fist, as if once more the unsubdued
Beasts shivering and docile stood

Like us before him. Do you remember how
A small brown pony would
Nuzzle the cube of sugar from your hand?

Broken from his mild reprimand
In fire and fury hard upon the taste
Of a sweet license, even these have raced

Uncurbed in us, where fires are fanned.

A NARROW ESCAPE

During a lull at dinner the vampire frankly
Confessed herself a symbol of the inner
Adventure. An old anxiousness took hold
Like a mesmerist hissing for each of us
To call up flitterings from within,
Crags and grottos, an olive dark that lured
Casements to loosen gleamings onto the Rhine.
More fluently than water she controlled
The vista. Later, von Blon said he had known
Her expressionless face before, her raven braids
—But where? A tale . . . a mezzotint? The tone
Was that of an 1830 pianoforte.
There followed for each a real danger of falling
Into the oubliette of that bland face,
Perfectly warned of how beneath it lay
The bat's penchant for sleeping all day long
Then flying off upon the wildest tangents
With little self-preserving shrieks, also
For ghastly scenes over letters and at meals,
Not to speak of positive evil, those nightly
Drainings of one's life, the blood, the laugh,
The cries for pardon, the indifferences—
And all performed with such a virtuoso's
Detachment from say their grandmothers' experience
That men in clubs would snort incredulously
Provided one escaped to tell the story.
It was then Charles thought to wonder, peering over
The rests of venison, what on earth a vampire
Means by the inner adventure. Her retort
Is now a classic in our particular circle.

SALOME

1

No wonder, shaggy saint, breast-deep in Jordan's
    Reflected gliding gardens,
That you assumed their swift compulsions sacred;
Nor that, dreaming you drank, so cool the water,
Regeneration, of which the first taste maddens,
    You let spill on the naked
  Stranger a pure and tripled mitre;

Nor that later, brooding on the sacrament
    Of flowing streams, you went
Back where none flow, and went in a new dread
Of water's claspings, whose rapt robe, whose crown
Make beggar and prince alike magnificent.
    A dry voice inside said,
  "Life is a pool in which we drown."

Finally then, small wonder the small king,
    Your captor, slavering
In a gold litter, bitten to the bone
By what would be, pretended not to hear
His veiled wild daughter sinuous on a string
    Of motives all her own
  Summon the executioner.

2

Our neighbors' little boy ran out to greet
    The chow, his runaway pet,
And was fearfully mauled. Breaking its mouth on fences
Down the struck street the orange mad dog tore
Until my father's pistol made of it
    Pinks, reds, a thrash of senses
  Outside the stationery store.

I was crying, but stayed on to watch. I saw
    The swelled tongue, the black maw,
And had seen earlier this meek dog trot off

Into the brambles of a vacant lot,
Suspecting then what I now know as law:
    That you can have enough
    Of human love. The chow forgot

The dim back porch, whistle and waterbowl;
    Confessing with a growl
How sweetly they subdued, forgot caresses;
Began to suffer the exactitude
Of its first nature, which was animal.
    Back in the child's oasis
    It told what it had understood.

3
The camel's vast thirst is the needle's eye.
    Whosoever faithfully
Desires desire more than its object shall
Find his right heaven, be he saint or brute.
But in a child's delirium never he
    Who next appears, the hale
    Young doctor from the Institute,

Atwirl like some exalted princess, or
    The ego of Pasteur,
Imperious for prophetic heads to probe
Upon a platter. "Ha!" he cries, "this brow
Swaddles a tangleworld I must explore!
    Stout vein and swaying lobe
    Redden beneath my knives. And now

Let chattering apes, let the last proud birds screech
    Abuse, well out of reach—"
Or later, quiet, drinks in the hiss and hurl
Of burning issues down to a pronged pool
Soon parched, mere clay, whose littlest crown ableach
    Suns lighten and winds whirl
    Back into earth, the easier school.

MIRROR

I grow old under an intensity
Of questioning looks. *Nonsense,*
I try to say, *I cannot teach you children
How to live.—If not you, who will?*
Cries one of them aloud, grasping my gilded
Frame till the world sways. *If not you, who will?*
Between their visits the table, its arrangement
Of Bible, fern and Paisley, all past change,
Does very nicely. If ever I feel curious
As to what others endure,
Across the parlor *you* provide examples,
Wide open, sunny, of everything I am
Not. You embrace a whole world without once caring
To set it in order. That takes thought. Out there
Something is being picked. The red-and-white bandannas
Go to my heart. A fine young man
Rides by on horseback. Now the door shuts. Hester
Confides in me her first unhappiness.
This much, you see, would never have been fitted
Together, but for me. Why then is it
They more and more neglect me? Late one sleepless
Midsummer night I strained to keep
Five tapers from your breathing. *No,* the widowed
Cousin said, *let them go out.* I did.
The room brimmed with gray sound, all the instreaming
Muslin of your dream . . .
Years later now, two of the grown grandchildren
Sit with novels face-down on the sill,
Content to muse upon your tall transparence,
Your clouds, brown fields, persimmon far
And cypress near. One speaks. *How superficial
Appearances are!* Since then, as if a fish
Had broken the perfect silver of my reflectiveness,
I have lapses. I suspect
Looks from behind, where nothing is, cool gazes

Mirror

Through the blind flaws of my mind. As days,
As decades lengthen, this vision
Spreads and blackens. I do not know whose it is,
But I think it watches for my last silver
To blister, flake, float leaf by life, each milling-
Downward dumb conceit, to a standstill
From which not even you strike any brilliant
Chord in me, and to a faceless will,
Echo of mine, I am amenable.

AMSTERDAM

'Au pays qui te ressemble'

There is a city whose fair houses wizen
In a strict web of streets, of waterways
In which the clock tower gurgles and sways,
And there desire is freed from the body's prison.

Into a black impasse deep in the maze
A mirror thrusts her brilliant severed head,
Mouth red and moist, and pale curls diamonded.
A youth advances towards the wraith, delays,

Squints through the window at a rumpled bed,
Cat, the familiar, lolling on batik,
The leman's person now no more unique
Than any hovel uninhabited,

Then turns, leaving her wrappered in a reek
Of realism, back the way he came.
Her jewels rekindle in their sooty frame
Lights for a future sleuth of the oblique.

(Once, once only to have laid absolute claim
Upon that love long held in readiness,
Not by the flesh in any stale undress,
Nor by the faithful ghost whose lips inflame

Lips curling dry, licked once to evanesce;
One night one autumn, so to have taken hold
Of certain volumes violent yet controlled
As to leave nothing for regret, unless

A strand of hair, pale auburn not quite gold
On the creased cushion, being what you must bear,
Guided the passion to its hush, like prayer,
And paler, cooler, tapered, as foretold,

Amsterdam

Into the sheer gold of nobody's hair,
The fragrance of whatever we suppose
Wafted, as music over water flows
Into the darkened sleeper, now elsewhere . . .)

Next day, is it myself whose image those
Sunning their own on the canal's far side
Are smiling to see reel at the downglide
Of one leaf, wallow, painfully recompose?

My head has fallen forward open-eyed.
Word of somebody's Schumann—"like a swan
That breasts a torrent of obsidian"—
Idles below me in formaldehyde.

Have I become my senses, all else gone?
A warm gust from the luxurious act
Interrupts reflection, leaves it tracked
With dust, like water sunlight moves upon.

By dark the world is once again intact,
Or so the mirrors, wiped clean, try to reason . . .
O little moons, misshapen but arisen
To blind with the emotions they refract!

THREE CHORES

1. WATER BOILING

When Polly's reddening hand
Let fall into the kettle
The greenest few of all
Her backyard's victuals

Which early underground
Imbibed from the hot metals
A cooking lacking little
To set them on her table

How while each knowing bubble
Jolted ebulliently
Good it felt to be going
At last where the ideal

Erupting of an eyeball
That dwelt more than its fill
On summer's flame shall scour
The kitchen from the hill!

2. NIGHT LAUNDRY

Of daily soilure laving
Fabric of all and sundry
With no time for believing
Loving might work the wonder

Who among clouded linen
Has scattered blueing then
Well over wrist in grieving
Dismissed all but the doing

Three Chores

May see to clotheslines later
A week of swans depending
From wooden beaks take flight
Flapping at dawn from water's

Jewel of the first water
And every dismal matter's
Absorption in its cleansing
Bring the new day to light.

3. ITALIAN LESSON

It will not do Luigi
You in this fireless room
Tirelessly expounding
The sense of so much sound

As if to speak were rather
Those promenades in Rome
Where each cool eye plays moth
To flames largely its own

Than the resounding Latin
Catacomb or labyrinth
Corinthian overgrown
With French sphinx or the heated tones

Of all these quenched at nightfall
Yet sparkling on a lip
At whose mute call I turn
To certain other lessons hard to learn.

MARSYAS

I used to write in the café sometimes:
Poems on menus, read all over town
Or talked out before ever written down.
One day a girl brought in his latest book.
I opened it—stiff rhythms, gorgeous rhymes—
And made a face. Then crash! my cup upset.
Of twenty upward looks mine only met
His, that gold archaic lion's look

Wherein I saw my wiry person skinned
Of every skill it labored to acquire
And heard the plucked nerve's elemental twang.
They found me dangling where his golden wind
Inflicted so much music on the lyre
That no one could have told you what he sang.

ORFEO

Ah downward through the dark coulisse,
Impelled to walk the stage of hell,
Unwind as in a theater gilt and puce
His opulence of pain until

Each damned soul dropped its trembling fan
(Which in the gusts of wooing trembled still)
And wept to hear him: it was then
Sickeningly he divined, but with an odd thrill,

Among the shadows of a box
That brow, that hand outspread upon
The plush worn bare, a white peacock's
Genius at dusk on a dissolving lawn,

Her loss within his music's rise and fall
Having become perpetual.

THE DOODLER

Most recent in the long race that descends
From me, welcome! and least askew of ikons
That grow on a new page like rapid lichens
Among the telephone numbers of new friends.

These I commune with every day. Hellos,
Goodbyes. Often by dusk a pair of eyes
Is all I draw; the pencil stupefies
Their lids with kohl until they almost close

But then do not, as if, more animate
Than any new friend's voice flattened by news,
Guessing some brilliant function I refuse,
And why, and wanting to accept their fate.

Noses as yet, alas, revert to profile.
Lips, too, are pursed in this or that direction,
Or raised to other lips from sheer distraction;
To mine, not once. While still, just as at Deauville

Off-season, tiny hands are better hidden
By great muffs of albino porcupine.
Indeed, nothing I do is at all fine
Save certain abstract forms. These come unbidden:

Stars, oblongs linked, or a baroque motif
Expressed so forcibly that it indents
A blank horizon generations hence
With signs and pressures, massing to relief

Like thunderheads one day in sultry foretaste
Of flashes first envisioned as your own
When, squat and breathless, you inscribe on stone
Your names for me, my inkling of an artist—

The Doodler

He-Who-endures-the-disembodied-Voice
Or *Who-in-wrath-puts-down-the-Black-Receiver*—
And, more than image then, a rain, a river
Of prescience, you reflect and I rejoice!

Far, far behind already is that aeon
Of pin-heads, bodies each a ragged weevil,
Slit-mouthed and spider-leggèd, with eyes like gravel,
Wavering under trees of purple crayon.

Shapes never realized, were you dogs or chairs?
That page is brittle now, if not long burned.
This morning's little boy stands (I have learned
To do feet) gazing down a flight of stairs.

And when A calls to tell me he enjoyed
The evening, I begin again. Again
Emerge, O sunbursts, garlands, creatures, men,
Ever more lifelike out of the white void!

ABOUT THE PHOENIX

But in the end one tires of the high-flown.
If it were simply a matter of life or death
We should by now welcome the darkening room,
Wrinkling of linen, window at last violet,
The rosy body in its chair, relaxed,
And then the appearance of unsuspected lights.
We should walk wonderingly into that other world
With its red signs pulsing and long lit lanes.
But often at nightfall, ambiguous
As the city itself, a giant jeweled bird
Comes cawing to the sill, dispersing thought
Like a bird-bath, and with such final barbarity
As to wear thin at once terror and novelty.
So that a sumptuous monotony
Sets in, a pendulum of amethysts
In the shape of a bird, keyed up for ever fiercer
Flights between ardor and ashes, back and forth;
Caught in whose talons any proof of grace,
Even your face, particularly your face
Fades, featureless in flame, or wan, a fading
Tintype of some cooling love, according
To the creature's whim. And in the end, despite
Its pyrotechnic curiosity, the process
Palls. One night
Your body winces grayly from its chair,
Embarks, a tearful child, to rest
On the dark breast of the fulfilled past.
The first sleep here is the sleep fraught
As never before with densities, plume, oak,
Black water, a blind flapping. And you wake
Unburdened, look about for friends—but O
Could not even the underworld forego
The publishing of omens, naively?
Nothing requires you to make sense of them
And yet you shiver from the dim clay shore,

Gazing. There in the lake, four rows of stilts
Rise, a first trace of culture, shy at dawn
Though blackened as if forces long confined
Had smouldered and blazed forth. In the museum
You draw back lest the relics of those days
—A battered egg cup and a boat with feet—
Have lost their glamour. They have not. The guide
Fairly exudes his tale of godless hordes
Sweeping like clockwork over Switzerland,
Till what had been your very blood ticks out
Voluptuous homilies. Ah, how well one might,
If it were less than a matter of life or death,
Traffic in strong prescriptions, "live" and "die"!
But couldn't the point about the phoenix
Be not agony or resurrection, rather
A mortal lull that followed either,
During which flames expired as they should,
And dawn, discovering ashes not yet stirred,
Buildings in rain, but set on rock,
Beggar and sparrow entertaining one another,
Showed me your face, for that moment neither
Alive nor dead, but turned in sleep
Away from whatever waited to be endured?

VOICES FROM THE OTHER WORLD

Presently at our touch the teacup stirred,
Then circled lazily about
From A to Z. The first voice heard
(If they are voices, these mute spellers-out)
Was that of an engineer

Originally from Cologne.
Dead in his 22nd year
Of cholera in Cairo, he had KNOWN
NO HAPPINESS. He once met Goethe, though.
Goethe had told him: PERSEVERE.

Our blind hound whined. With that, a horde
Of voices gathered above the Ouija board,
Some childish and, you might say, blurred
By sleep; one little boy
Named Will, reluctant possibly in a ruff

Like a large-lidded page out of El Greco, pulled
Back the arras for that next voice,
Cold and portentous: ALL IS LOST.
FLEE THIS HOUSE. OTTO VON THURN UND TAXIS.
OBEY. YOU HAVE NO CHOICE.

Frightened, we stopped; but tossed
Till sunrise striped the rumpled sheets with gold.
Each night since then, the moon waxes,
Small insects flit round a cold torch
We light, that sends them pattering to the porch . . .

But no real Sign. New voices come,
Dictate addresses, begging us to write;
Some warn of lives misspent, and all of doom
In ways that so exhilarate
We are sleeping sound of late.

Last night the teacup shattered in a rage.
Indeed, we have grown nonchalant
Towards the other world. In the gloom here,
Our elbows on the cleared
Table, we talk and smoke, pleased to be stirred

Rather by buzzings in the jasmine, by the drone
Of our own voices and poor blind Rover's wheeze,
Than by those clamoring overhead,
Obsessed or piteous, for a commitment
We still have wit to postpone

Because, once looked at lit
By the cold reflections of the dead
Risen extinct but irresistible,
Our lives have never seemed more full, more real,
Nor the full moon more quick to chill.

DREAM
(ESCAPE FROM THE SCULPTURE
MUSEUM)
AND WAKING

Softening the marbles, day
Is dawning, which two elms vein.
Presently, slow as crochet,
White veils grow across the scene.
Now that my life has lost its way
I watch for it, through a cold pane

Out past all this eloquence
Inside: look, gesture, flowing raiment
Done in porphyry or jasper whence
One white arm, for a long moment
Raised to strike, relents
(Not to spoil one's enjoyment)

Back into stone, back into being
Hard, handsome to the fingertips,
With eyes that bulge unseeing
To call down an immaculate eclipse
Upon the world. It began snowing
Because of the statues, perhaps.

Or because for a long time now
I have wanted to be more natural
Than they, to issue forth anew
In a profusion inimitable
As it is chaste and quickly through.
White void, my heart grows full

With all you have undone!
Starwise, from coldest heights, a gong
Of silence strikes *end of an aeon,*
Reverberates keen and strong
Until a far veil lifts. Someone
Is stumbling this way. Neither young

Dream (Escape from the Sculpture Museum) and Waking

Nor old, man nor woman, so
Propelled by cold, a human figure
Barely begun, a beggar, no,
Two by now, and ever nearer, bigger,
Cause me to stiffen in a show
Of being human also, eager

For what never, never occurs.
In the tradition of their kind
Exhaustingly the wayfarers
Breathe out white and pass by blind.
After them trot two ermine-yellow curs.
These look up, almost lag behind,

Then follow with two unheard shakes
Of bells. As my eyes close, nearby
Something unwinds and breaks.
Perhaps the Discus Thrower has let fly
Or Laocoön stepped from his snakes
Like old clothes. The scene changes. I

Am mounted in a village common.
A child calls. Early lamps and sunset
Stream together down the snowman's
Face and dazzle in his jet
Eyes. He lives, but melts. I summon
All my strength. I wake in a cold sweat.

You are beside me. It is dawn
In a friend's house in late
Summer. I softly rise, put on
A robe, and by the misty light
Watch you sleep. You moan
Once in your own dream, and are quiet.

I turn to look outdoors
At the formal garden our friend made.
A figure kneels among the flowers,

50

A limestone river-god,
Arm raised so that a clear stream pours
From the urn level with his head.

But a white, eyeless shape
Is gesturing deep in my dream.
I turn back to you for companionship.
At once there rises like perfume
To numb me, from your too heavy sleep,
What we said last night in this room—

All of it muffled to protect
Our sleeping friend—when for a wild
Half-hour the light burned, the clock ticked.
You called me cold, I said you were a child.
I said we must respect
Each other's solitude. You *smiled*.

Well, I shall wake you now,
Smiling myself to hide my fear.
Sun turns the stone urn's overflow
To fire. If I had missed before
The relevance of the road in snow,
The little dogs, the blinded pair,

I judge it now in your slow eyes
Which meet mine, fill with things
We do not name, then fill with the sunrise
And close, because too much light stings,
All the more when shed on these
Our sleeps of stone, our wakenings.

IN THE HALL OF MIRRORS

The parquet barely gleams, a lake.
The windows weaken the dark trees.
The mirrors to their bosoms take
Far glints of water, which they freeze
And wear like necklaces.

Some pause in front of others with
Glimmers of mutual admiration.
Even to draw breath is uncouth.
Steps make the silver marrow spin
Up and down every spine.

You feel that something must begin.
To clickings from the chandeliers
A woman and a man come in
And creak about. She sighs, he peers.
A guide hisses in their ears,

"Your seeresses of sheer Space
In argent colloquy despise
Anything personal or commonplace."
Looked at, the mirrors close their eyes.
Through the guide's good offices

In one glass brow a tree is lit
That multiplies itself in tiers,
Tempting the pair to populate
Those vistas from which visitors
Ricochet in fours,

Eights, sixteens, till the first two gaze
At one another through a glazed crush
Of their own kind, and the man says,
"Complex but unmysterious,
This is no life for us."

He shuts the camera whose cold eye
Far outshone his own or hers.
The woman, making no reply,
Scans the remotest mirrors within mirrors
For grander figures,

Not just those of herself and him
Repeated soothingly, as though
Somebody's wits were growing dim—
Those! those beyond! The guide says, "Time to go."
They turn to do so,

And of a million likenesses
The two had thought to leave behind
Not one but nimble as you please
Turns with them, masterfully aligned.
Then all slip out of mind

And in the solitary hall
The lobes of crystal gather dust.
From glass to glass an interval
Widens like moonrise over frost
No tracks have ever crossed.

A DEDICATION

Hans, there are moments when the whole mind
Resolves into a pair of brimming eyes, or lips
Parting to drink from the deep spring of a death
That freshness they do not yet need to understand.
These are the moments, if ever, an angel steps
Into the mind, as kings into the dress
Of a poor goatherd, for their acts of charity.
There are moments when speech is but a mouth pressed
Lightly and humbly against the angel's hand.

From Water Street *(1962)*

AN URBAN CONVALESCENCE

Out for a walk, after a week in bed,
I find them tearing up part of my block
And, chilled through, dazed and lonely, join the dozen
In meek attitudes, watching a huge crane
Fumble luxuriously in the filth of years.
Her jaws dribble rubble. An old man
Laughs and curses in her brain,
Bringing to mind the close of *The White Goddess*.

As usual in New York, everything is torn down
Before you have had time to care for it.
Head bowed, at the shrine of noise, let me try to recall
What building stood here. Was there a building at all?
I have lived on this same street for a decade.

Wait. Yes. Vaguely a presence rises
Some five floors high, of shabby stone
—Or am I confusing it with another one
In another part of town, or of the world?—
And over its lintel into focus vaguely
Misted with blood (my eyes are shut)
A single garland sways, stone fruit, stone leaves,
Which years of grit had etched until it thrust
Roots down, even into the poor soil of my seeing.
When did the garland become part of me?
I ask myself, amused almost,
Then shiver once from head to toe,

Transfixed by a particular cheap engraving of garlands
Bought for a few francs long ago,
All calligraphic tendril and cross-hatched rondure,
Ten years ago, and crumpled up to stanch
Boughs dripping, whose white gestures filled a cab,
And thought of neither then nor since.
Also, to clasp them, the small, red-nailed hand

Of no one I can place. Wait. No. Her name, her features
Lie toppled underneath that year's fashions.
The words she must have spoken, setting her face
To fluttering like a veil, I cannot hear now,
Let alone understand.

So that I am already on the stair,
As it were, of where I lived,
When the whole structure shudders at my tread
And soundlessly collapses, filling
The air with motes of stone.
Onto the still erect building next door
Are pressed levels and hues—
Pocked rose, streaked greens, brown whites.
Who drained the pousse-café?
Wires and pipes, snapped off at the roots, quiver.

Well, that is what life does. I stare
A moment longer, so. And presently
The massive volume of the world
Closes again.

Upon that book I swear
To abide by what it teaches:
Gospels of ugliness and waste,
Of towering voids, of soiled gusts,
Of a shrieking to be faced
Full into, eyes astream with cold—

With cold?
All right then. With self-knowledge.

Indoors at last, the pages of *Time* are apt
To open, and the illustrated mayor of New York,
Given a glimpse of how and where I work,
To note yet one more house that can be scrapped.

Unwillingly I picture
My walls weathering in the general view.
It is not even as though the new
Buildings did very much for architecture.

Suppose they did. The sickness of our time requires
That these as well be blasted in their prime.
You would think the simple fact of having lasted
Threatened our cities like mysterious fires.

There are certain phrases which to use in a poem
Is like rubbing silver with quicksilver. Bright
But facile, the glamour deadens overnight.
For instance, how "the sickness of our time"

Enhances, then debases, what I feel.
At my desk I swallow in a glass of water
No longer cordial, scarcely wet, a pill
They had told me not to take until much later.

With the result that back into my imagination
The city glides, like cities seen from the air,
Mere smoke and sparkle to the passenger
Having in mind another destination

Which now is not that honey-slow descent
Of the Champs-Elysées, her hand in his,
But the dull need to make some kind of house
Out of the life lived, out of the love spent.

FROM A NOTEBOOK

The whiteness near and far.
The cold, the hush. . . .
A first word stops
The blizzard, steps
Out into fresh
Candor. You ask no more.

Each never taken stride
Leads onward, though
In circles ever
Smaller, smaller.
The vertigo
Upholds you. And now to glide

Across the frozen pond,
Steelshod, to chase
Its dreamless oval
With loop and spiral
Until (your face
Downshining, lidded, drained

Of any need to know
What hid, what called,
Wisdom or error,
Beneath that mirror)
The page you scrawled
Turns. A new day. Fresh snow.

A VISION OF THE GARDEN

One winter morning as a child
Upon the windowpane's thin frost I drew
Forehead and eyes and mouth the clear and mild
Features of nobody I knew

And then abstracted looking through
This or that wet transparent line
Beyond beheld a winter garden so
Heavy with snow its hedge of pine

And sun so brilliant on the snow
I breathed my pleasure out onto the chill pane
Only to see its angel fade in mist.
I was a child, I did not know

That what I longed for would resist
Neither what cold lines should my finger trace
On colder grounds before I found anew
In yours the features of that face

Whose words whose looks alone undo
Such frosts I lay me down in love in fear
At how they melt become a blossoming pear
Joy outstretched in our bodies' place.

AFTER GREECE

Light into the olive entered
And was oil. Rain made the huge pale stones
Shine from within. The moon turned his hair white
Who next stepped from between the columns,
Shielding his eyes. All through
The countryside were old ideas
Found lying open to the elements.
Of the gods' houses only
A minor premise here and there
Would be balancing the heaven of fixed stars
Upon a Doric capital. The rest
Lay spilled, their fluted drums half sunk in cyclamen
Or deep in water's biting clarity
Which just barely upheld me
The next week, when I sailed for home.
But where is home—these walls?
These limbs? The very spaniel underfoot
Races in sleep, toward what?
It is autumn. I did not invite
Those guests, windy and brittle, who drink my liquor.
Returning from a walk I find
The bottles filled with spleen, my room itself
Smeared by reflection onto the far hemlocks.
I some days flee in dream
Back to the exposed porch of the maidens
Only to find my great-great-grandmothers
Erect there, peering
Into a globe of red Bohemian glass.
As it swells and sinks, I call up
Graces, Furies, Fates, removed
To my country's warm, lit halls, with rivets forced
Through drapery, and nothing left to bear.
They seem anxious to know
What holds up heaven nowadays.
I start explaining how in that vast fire

Were other irons—well, Art, Public Spirit,
Ignorance, Economics, Love of Self,
Hatred of Self, a hundred more,
Each burning to be felt, each dedicated
To sparing us the worst; how I distrust them
As I should have done those ladies; how I want
Essentials: salt, wine, olive, the light, the scream—
No! I have scarcely named you,
And look, in a flash you stand full-grown before me,
Row upon row, Essentials,
Dressed like your sister caryatids
Or tombstone angels jealous of their dead,
With undulant coiffures, lips weathered, cracked by grime,
And faultless eyes gone blank beneath the immense
Zinc and gunmetal northern sky . . .
Stay then. Perhaps the system
Calls for spirits. This first glass I down
To the last time
I ate and drank in that old world. May I
Also survive its meanings, and my own.

PRISM

a paperweight

Having lately taken up residence
In a suite of chambers
Windless, compact and sunny, ideal
Lodging for the pituitary gland of Euclid
If not for a "single gentleman (references),"
You have grown used to the playful inconveniences,
The floors that slide from under you helter-skelter,
Invisible walls put up in mid-
Stride, leaving you warped for the rest of the day,
A spoon in water; also that pounce
Of wild color from corner to page,
Straightway consuming the latter
Down to your very signature,
After which there is nothing to do but retire,
Licking the burn, into—into—
Look: (Heretofore
One could have said where one was looking,
In or out. But now it almost—) Look,
You dreamed of this:
To fuse in borrowed fires, to drown
In depths that were not there. You meant
To rest your bones in a maroon plush box,
Doze the old vaudeville out, of mind and object,
Little foreseeing their effect on you,
Those dagger-eyed insatiate performers
Who from the first false insight
To the most recent betrayal of outlook,
Crystal, hypnotic atom,
Have held you rapt, the proof, the child
Wanted by neither. Now and then
It is given to see clearly. There
Is what remains of you, a body
Unshaven, flung on the sofa. Stains of egg

Harden about the mouth, smoke still
Rises between fingers or from nostrils.
The eyes deflect the stars through years of vacancy.
Your agitation at such moments
Is all too human. You and the stars
Seem both endangered, each
At the other's utter mercy. Yet the gem
Revolves in space, the vision shuttles off.
A toneless waltz glints through the pea-sized funhouse.
The day is breaking someone else's heart.

SCENES OF CHILDHOOD

for Claude Fredericks

My mother's lamp once out,
I press a different switch:
A field within the dim
White screen ignites,
Vibrating to the rapt
Mechanical racket
Of a real noon field's
Crickets and gnats.

And to its candid heart
I move with heart ajar,
With eyes that smart less
From pollen or heat
Than from the buried day
Now rising like a moon,
Shining, unwinding
Its taut white sheet.

Two or three bugs that lit
Earlier upon the blank
Sheen, all peaceable
Insensibility, drowse
As she and I cannot
Under the risen flood
Of thirty years ago—
A tree, a house

We had then, a late sun,
A door from which the primal
Figures jerky and blurred
As lightning bugs
From lanterns issue, next
To be taken for stars,
For fates. With knowing smiles
And beaded shrugs

My mother and two aunts
Loom on the screen. Their plucked
Brows pucker, their arms encircle
One another.
Their ashen lips move.
From the love seat's gloom
A quiet chuckle escapes
My white-haired mother

To see in that final light
A man's shadow mount
Her dress. And now she is
Advancing, sister-
less, but followed by
A fair child, or fury—
Myself at four, in tears.
I raise my fist,

Strike, she kneels down. The man's
Shadow afflicts us both.
Her voice behind me says
It might go slower.
I work dials, the film jams.
Our headstrong old projector
Glares at the scene which promptly
Catches fire.

Puzzled, we watch ourselves
Turn red and black, gone up
In a puff of smoke now coiling
Down fierce beams.
I switch them off. A silence.
Your father, she remarks,
Took those pictures; later
Says pleasant dreams,

Rises and goes. Alone
I gradually fade and cool.
Night scatters me with green
Rustlings, thin cries.
Out there between the pines
Have begun shining deeds,
Some low, inconstant (these
Would be fireflies),

Others as in high wind
Aflicker, staying lit.
There are nights we seem to ride
With cross and crown
Forth under them, through fumes,
Coils, the whole rattling epic—
Only to leap clear-eyed
From eiderdown,

Asleep to what we'd seen.
Father already fading—
Who focused your life long
Through little frames,
Whose microscope, now deep
In purple velvet, first
Showed me the skulls of flies,
The fur, the flames

Etching the jaws—father:
Shrunken to our true size.
Each morning, back of us,
Fields wail and shimmer.
To go out is to fall
Under fresh spells, cool web
And stinging song new-hatched
Each day, all summer.

A minute galaxy
About my head will easily
Needle me back. The day's
Inaugural *Damn*
Spoken, I start to run,
Inane, like them, but breathing
In and out the sun
And air I am.

The son and heir! In the dark
It makes me catch my breath
And hear, from upstairs, hers—
That faintest hiss
And slither, as of life
Escaping into space,
Having led its characters
To the abyss

Of night. Immensely still
The heavens glisten. One broad
Path of vague stars is floating
Off, a shed skin
Of all whose fine cold eyes
First told us, locked in ours:
You are the heroes without name
Or origin.

THE WORLD AND THE CHILD

Letting his wisdom be the whole of love,
The father tiptoes out, backwards. A gleam
Falls on the child awake and wearied of,

Then, as the door clicks shut, is snuffed. The glove-
Gray afterglow appalls him. It would seem
That letting wisdom be the whole of love

Were pastime even for the bitter grove
Outside, whose owl's white hoot of disesteem
Falls on the child awake and wearied of.

He lies awake in pain, he does not move,
He will not call. The women, hearing him,
Would let their wisdom be the whole of love.

People have filled the room he lies above.
Their talk, mild variation, chilling theme,
Falls on the child. Awake and wearied of

Mere pain, mere wisdom also, he would have
All the world waking from its winter dream,
Letting its wisdom be. The whole of love
Falls on the child awake and wearied of.

CHILDLESSNESS

The weather of this winter night, my dream-wife
Ranting and raining, wakes me. Her cloak blown back
To show the lining's dull lead foil
Sweeps along asphalt. Houses
Look blindly on; one glimmers through a blind.
Outside, I hear her tricklings
Arraign my little plot:
Had it or not agreed
To transplantation for the common good
Of certain rare growths yielding guaranteed
Gold pollen, gender of suns, large, hardy,
Enviable blooms? But in my garden
Nothing's been seeded. Neither
Is that glimmering window mine.
I lie and think about the rain,
How it has been drawn up from the impure ocean,
From gardens lightly, deliberately tainted;
How it falls back, time after time,
Through poisons visible at sunset
When the enchantress, masked as friend, unfurls
Entire bolts of voluminous pistachio,
Saffron, and rose.
These, as I fall back to sleep,
And other slow colors clothe me, glide
To rest, then burst along my limbs like buds,
Like bombs from the navigator's vantage,
Waking me, lulling me. Later I am shown
The erased metropolis reassembled
On sampans, freighted each
With toddlers, holy dolls, dead ancestors.
One tiny monkey puzzles over fruit.
The vision rises and falls, the garland
Gently takes root
In the sea's coma. Hours go by
Before I can stand to own

Childlessness

A sky stained red, a world
Clad only in rags, threadbare,
Dabbling the highway's ice with blood.
A world. The cloak thrown down for it to wear
In token of past servitude
Has fallen onto the shoulders of my parents
Whom it is eating to the bone.

ROGER CLAY'S PROPOSAL

I may be oversusceptible to news
But what I see in the papers leaves me numb.
The bomb. The ultimatum. Wires hum—
Adult impersonators giving interviews,

As if that helped. What would? I've thought of it.
With all due ceremony—flags unfurled,
Choirs, priests—the leaders of a sobered world
Should meet, kneel down, and, joining hands, submit

To execution: say in Rome or Nice—
Towns whose economy depends on crowds.
Ah, but those boys, their heads aren't in the clouds.
They would find reasons not to die for peace.

Damn them. I'd give *my* life. Each day I meet
Men like me, young, indignant. We're not cranks.
Will some of them step up? That's plenty. Thanks.
Now let's move before we get cold feet.

Music we'll need, and short, clear speeches given
Days of maximum coverage in the press.
We'll emphasize disinterestedness,
Drive the point home that someone could be driven

To do this. Where to go? Why not Japan,
Land of the honorable suicide.
And will the world change heart? Until we've tried,
No one can say it will not. No one can.

FIVE OLD FAVORITES

1. A DREAM OF OLD VIENNA

The mother sits, the whites of her eyes tinted
By a gas lamp of red Bohemian glass.
Her one gray lock could be a rosy fireworks.
She hums the galop from Lehár's Requiem Mass.

Deepening a blood-red handkerchief the father
Has drawn over his face, the warm beams wreathe
Its foldings into otherworldly features
Now and then stirred lightly from beneath.

The child, because of his extreme pallor,
Acquires a normal look as the lamp glows,
For which the mother is and is not grateful,
Torn between conflicting libidos.

To wed the son when he has slain the father,
Or thrust the brat *at once* into the damp . . . ?
Such are the throbbing issues that enliven
Many a cozy evening round the lamp.

2. THE MIDNIGHT SNACK

When I was little and he was riled
It never entered my father's head
Not to flare up, roar and turn red.
Mother kept cool and smiled.

Now every night I tiptoe straight
Through my darkened kitchen for
The refrigerator door—
It opens, the inviolate!

Illumined as in dreams I take
A glass of milk, a piece of cake,
Then stealthily retire,

Mindful of how the gas stove's black-
Browed pilot eye's blue fire
Burns into my turned back.

3. SUNDOWN AND STARLIGHT

He licks the tallest tree, and takes a bite.
His day's excess has left him flushed and limp. Then, too,
It is time she changed for the evening. Hadn't she better
Be thinking what to wear? Nothing seems quite

To match her mood. Women! She must consider
One dress after another of pale or fiery hue.
At the hour's end, as foreseen, her favorite dark blue
Comes fold by fold out of its chest of cedar.

His jaws have closed on the tree's base.
Moments like this, he turns into a compulsive eater.
Men! Let him burn all night. She has other things to do
Than care for him. She opens her jewel case.

4. EVENT WITHOUT PARTICULARS

Something will be hanging from the ceiling—
A dagger fern in chains? Shroud of a chandelier?
One feebly blinking bulb? Be that as it may,
Something you notice right away.

*Something will decorate the wall—*a calendar?
A looking glass? A scorched place? One never can say.
*And something lie on the table—*a teacup or book
You may care to read if you dare to look.

75

Then comes the opening of the door.
Somebody enters—young, face deep in a nosegay,
Or with a drink, or a crutch and milk-blind eyes.
In any case *you will rise*

And go to her over whatever is underfoot
To make you feel at home, since you have come to stay—
Black and white marble might be used for some;
For others, roses of linoleum.

5. THE DANDELION SERMON

In the heat of a sentence I stopped. You waited
Complacently, but the mind
Had been breathed upon at last.
Innumerable feathery particles rose in less than wind

Out over the nude waters where both suns
Fierily, the reflected and the seen,
Strove to be one, then perhaps were, within
A white haze not at once or ever with ease construed.

ANNIE HILL'S GRAVE

Amen. The casket like a spaceship bears her
In streamlined, airtight comfort underground.
Necropolis is a nice place to visit;
One would not want to live there all year round.

So think the children of its dead, emerging
From shadow by the small deep gates of clay,
Exclaiming softly, joyful if bewildered,
To see each other rouged, heads bald or gray.

Some have not met, though constant to the City,
For decades. Now their slowly sunnier
Counterclockwise movement, linked and loving,
Slackens the whirlpool that has swallowed her.

Alone, she grips, against confusion, pictures
Of us the living, and of the tall youth
She wed but has not seen for thirty summers.
Used to the dark, he lies in the next booth,

Part of that whole, poor, overpopulated
Land of our dreams, that "instant" space
—To have again, just add stars, wind, and water—
Shrinkingly broached. And, as the brief snail-trace

Of her withdrawal dries upon our faces
The silence drums into her upturned face.

ANGEL

Above my desk, whirring and self-important
(Though not much larger than a hummingbird)
In finely woven robes, school of Van Eyck,
Hovers a patently angelic visitor.
He points one index finger out the window
At winter snatching to its heart,
To crystal vacancy, the misty
Exhalations of houses and of people running home
From the cold sun pounding on the sea;
While with the other hand
He indicates the piano
Where the Sarabande No. 1 lies open
At a passage I shall never master
But which has already, and effortlessly, mastered me.
He drops his jaw as if to say, or sing,
"Between the world God made
And this music of Satie,
Each glimpsed through veils, but whole,
Radiant and willed,
Demanding praise, demanding surrender,
How can you sit there with your notebook?
What do you think you are doing?"
However he says nothing—wisely: I could mention
Flaws in God's world, or Satie's; and for that matter
How did he come by *his* taste for Satie?
Half to tease him, I turn back to my page,
Its phrases thus far clotted, unconnected.
The tiny angel shakes his head.
There is no smile on his round, hairless face.
He does not want even these few lines written.

TO A BUTTERFLY

Already in midsummer
I miss your feet and fur.
Poor simple creature that you were,
What have you become!

Your slender person curled
About an apple twig
Rebounding to the winds' clear jig
Gave up the world

In favor of obscene
Gray matter, rode that ark
Until (as at the chance remark
Of Father Sheen)

Shining awake to slough
Your old life. And soon four
Dapper stained glass windows bore
You up—*Enough*.

Goodness, how tired one grows
Just looking through a prism:
Allegory, symbolism.
I've tried, Lord knows,

To keep from seeing double,
Blushed for whenever I did,
Prayed like a boy my cheek be hid
By manly stubble.

I caught you in a net
And first pierced your disguise
How many years ago? Time flies,
I am not yet

To a Butterfly

Proof against rigmarole.
Those frail wings, those antennae!
The day you hover without any
Tincture of soul,

Red monarch, swallowtail,
Will be the day my own
Wiles gather dust. Each will have flown
The other's jail.

THE PARROT FISH

The shadow of the little fishing launch
Discreetly, inch by inch,
Crept after us on its belly over
The reef's uneven floor.

The motor gasped out drowsy vapor.
Seconds went by before
Anyone thought to interpret
The jingling of Inez's bracelet.

Chalk-violet, olive, all veils and sequins, a
Priestess out of the next Old Testament extravaganza,
With round gold eyes and minuscule buckteeth,
Up flaunted into death

The parrot fish. And for a full hour beat
Irregular, passionate
Tattoos from its casket lined with zinc.
Finally we understood, I think.

Ashore, the warm waves licked our feet.
One or two heavy chords the heat
Struck, set the white beach vibrating.
And throwing back its head the sea began to sing.

SWIMMING BY NIGHT

A light going out in the forehead
Of the house by the ocean,
Into warm black its feints of diamond fade.
Without clothes, without caution

Plunging past gravity—
Wait! Where before
Had been floating nothing, is a gradual body
Half remembered, astral with phosphor,

Yours, risen from its tomb
In your own mind,
Haunting nimbleness, glimmerings a random
Spell has kindled. So that, new-limned

By this weak lamp
The evening's alcohol will feed
Until the genie chilling bids you limp
Heavily over stones to bed,

You wear your master's robe
One last time, the far break
Of waves, their length and sparkle, the spinning globe
You wear, and the star running down his cheek.

THE SMILE

It was going to rain.
Beneath his scalp
The silver ached. He got
With no one's help
To his feet. A cane
Steadied him up the stair.

It was warm there
On the sleeping porch.
His jacket hung
Over a chair would not
Let go his form.
He placed his round gold watch,

Unwound, among
Dimes, quarters, lunatic change . . .
He woke in bed,
Missing his spectacles.
He felt the strange
Palms laid on his forehead.

Then he heard other palms
Rattling in wind.
More time passed. He had dreams.
In one, rain fell
And fell, and when
The sun rose near at hand

Stood his life gleaming full.
The bubble-beaded
Tumbler magnified
A false and grinning friend
No longer needed.
He turned his face and died.

FOR PROUST

Over and over something would remain
Unbalanced in the painful sum of things.
Past midnight you arose, rang for your things.
You had to go into the world again.

You stop for breath outside the lit hotel,
A thin spoon bitter stimulants will stir.
Jean takes your elbow, Jacques your coat. The stir
Spreads—you are known to all the personnel—

As through packed public rooms you press (impending
Palms, chandeliers, orchestras, more palms,
The fracas and the fragrance) until your palms
Are moist with fear that you will miss the friend

Conjured—but she is waiting: a child still
At first glance, hung with fringes, on the low
Ottoman. In a voice reproachful and low
She says she understands you have been ill.

And you, because your time is running out,
Laugh in denial and begin to phrase
Your questions. There had been a little phrase
She hummed, you could not sleep tonight without

Hearing again. Then, of that day she had sworn
To come, and did not, was evasive later,
Would she not speak the truth two decades later,
From loving-kindness learned if not inborn?

She treats you to a look you cherished, light,
Bold: "Mon ami, how did we get along
At all, those years?" But in her hair a long
White lock has made its truce with appetite.

And presently she rises. Though in pain
You let her leave—the loved one always leaves.
What of the little phrase? Its notes, like leaves
In the strong tea you have contrived to drain,

Strangely intensify what you must do.
Back where you came from, up the strait stair, past
All understanding, bearing the whole past,
Your eyes grown wide and dark, eyes of a Jew,

You make for one dim room without contour
And station yourself there, beyond the pale
Of cough or of gardenia, erect, pale.
What happened is becoming literature.

Feverish in time, if you suspend the task,
An old, old woman shuffling in to draw
Curtains, will read a line or two, withdraw.
The world will have put on a thin gold mask.

A TENANCY

for David Jackson

Something in the light of this March afternoon
Recalls that first and dazzling one
Of 1946. I sat elated
In my old clothes, in the first of several
Furnished rooms, head cocked for the kind of sound
That is recognized only when heard.
A fresh snowfall muffled the road, unplowed
To leave blanker and brighter
The bright, blank page turned overnight.

A yellow pencil in midair
Kept sketching unfamiliar numerals,
The 9 and 6 forming a stereoscope
Through which to seize the Real
Old-Fashioned Winter of my landlord's phrase,
Through which the ponderous idées reçues
Of oak, velour, crochet, also the mantel's
Baby figures, value told me
In some detail at the outset, might be plumbed
For signs I should not know until I saw them.

But the objects, innocent
(As we all once were) of annual depreciation,
The more I looked grew shallower,
Pined under a luminous plaid robe
Thrown over us by the twin mullions, sashes,
And unequal oblong panes
Of windows and storm windows. These,
Washed in a rage, then left to dry unpolished,
Projected onto the inmost wall
Ghosts of the storm, like pebbles under water.

And indeed, from within, ripples
Of heat had begun visibly bearing up and away

86

The bouquets and wreathes of a quarter century.
Let them go, what did I want with them?
It was time to change that wallpaper!
Brittle, sallow in the new radiance,
Time to set the last wreath floating out
Above the dead, to sweep up flowers. The dance
Had ended, it was light; the men looked tired
And awkward in their uniforms.
I sat, head thrown back, and with the dried stains
Of light on my own cheeks, proposed
This bargain with—say with the source of light:
That given a few years more
(Seven or ten or, what seemed vast, fifteen)
To spend in love, in a country not at war,
I would give in return
All I had. All? A little sun
Rose in my throat. The lease was drawn.

I did not even feel the time expire.

I feel it though, today, in this new room,
Mine, with my things and thoughts, a view
Of housetops, treetops, the walls bare.
A changing light is deepening, is changing
To a gilt ballroom chair a chair
Bound to break under someone before long.
I let the light change also me.
The body that lived through that day
And the sufficient love and relative peace
Of those short years, is now not mine.
Would it be called a soul?
It knows, at any rate,
That when the light dies and the bell rings
Its leaner veteran will rise to face
Partners not recognized
Until drunk young again and gowned in changing
Flushes; and strains will rise,

A Tenancy

The bone-tipped baton beating, rapid, faint,
From the street below, from my depressions—

From the doorbell which rings.
One foot asleep, I hop
To let my three friends in. They stamp
Themselves free of the spring's
Last snow—or so we hope.

One has brought violets in a pot;
The second, wine; the best,
His open, empty hand. Now in the room
The sun is shining like a lamp.
I put the flowers where I need them most

And then, not asking why they come,
Invite the visitors to sit.
If I am host at last
It is of little more than my own past.
May others be at home in it.

From Nights and Days (1966)

NIGHTGOWN

A cold so keen,
My speech unfurls tonight
As from the chattering teeth
Of a sewing machine.

Whom words appear to warm,
Dear heart, wear mine. Come forth
Wound in their flimsy white
And give it form.

THE THOUSAND AND SECOND NIGHT

for Irma Brandeis

I. RIGOR VITAE

Istanbul. 21 March. I woke today
With an absurd complaint. The whole right half
Of my face refuses to move. I have to laugh
Watching the rest of it reel about in dismay

Under the double burden, while its twin
Sags on, though sentient, stupefied.
I'm here alone. Not quite—through fog outside
Loom wingèd letters: PAN AMERICAN.

Twenty-five hundred years this city has stood between
The passive Orient and our frantic West.
I see no reason to be depressed;
There are too many other things I haven't seen,

Like Hagia Sophia. Tea drunk, shaved and dressed . . .
Dahin! Dahin!

The house of Heavenly Wisdom first became
A mosque, is now a flame-
less void. The apse,
Militantly dislocated,
Still wears those dark-green epaulettes
On which (to the pilgrim who forgets
His Arabic) a wild script of gold whips
Has scribbled glowering, dated
Slogans: "God is my grief!" perhaps,
Or "Byzantine,
Go home!"

Above you, the great dome,
Bald of mosaic, senile, floated
In a gilt wash. Its old profusion's
Hypnotic shimmer, back and forth between
That of the abacus, that of the nebula,
Had been picked up from the floor,
The last of numberless handfuls,
By the last 18th century visitor.
You did not want to think of yourself for once,
But you had held your head erect
Too many years within such transcendental skulls
As this one not to feel the usual, if no
Longer flattering kinship. You'd let go
Learning and faith as well, you too had wrecked
Your precious sensibility. What else did you expect?

Outdoors. Uprooted, turban-crested stones
Lie side by side. It's as I might have feared.
The building, desperate for youth, has smeared
All over its original fine bones

Acres of ochre plaster. A diagram
Indicates how deep in the mudpack
The real façade is. I want *my* face back.
A pharmacist advises

The Hamam

After the hour of damp heat
One is addressed in gibberish, shown
Into a marble cell and thrown
On marble, there to be scrubbed clean,

Is wrapped in towels and a sheet
And led upstairs to this lean tomb
Made all of panes (red, amber, green)
With a glass star hung in the gloom,

The Thousand and Second Night

Here sits effaced by gemlike moods,
Tastes neither coffee nor loukoum,
And to the attendant who intrudes

(Or archeologist or thief)
Gravely uptilts one's mask of platinum
Still dripping, in a sign of life.

And now what? Back, I guess, to the modern town.
Midway across the bridge, an infantile
Memory promises to uncramp my style.
I stop in deepening light to jot it down:

On the crest of her wrist, by the black watered silk of the watch-
band, his grandmother had a wen, a hard mauve bubble up
from which bristled three or four white hairs. How often he had
lain in her lap and been lulled to a rhythm easily the whole
world's then—the yellowish sparkle of a ring marking its outer
limit, while in the foreground, silhouetted like the mosque of
Suleiman the Magnificent, mass and minarets felt by someone
fallen asleep on the deck of his moored caïque, that principal
landmark's rise and fall distinguished, from any other, her be-
loved hand.

Cold. A wind rising. An entire city
Dissolved by rhetoric. And out there, past
The mirror of the Bosporos, what black coast
Reflecting us into immobility?

On this side, crowds, a magic-lantern beam—
Belgians on bicycles, housewives with red hair,
Masts, cries of crows blown high in the rose-blue air,
Atatürk's tailcoat . . . It is like a dream,

The "death-in-life and life-in-death" of Yeats'
Byzantium; and if so, by the same token,
Alone in the sleepwalking scene, my flesh has woken
And sailed for the fixed shore beyond the straits.

2. THE CURE

The doctor recommended cortisone,
Diathermy, vitamins, and rest.
It worked. These months in Athens, no one's guessed
My little drama; I appear my own

Master again. However, once you've cracked
That so-called mirror of the soul,
It is not readily, if at all, made whole.
("Between the motion and the act

Falls the Shadow"—T. S. Eliot.)
Part of me has remained cold and withdrawn.
The day I went up to the Parthenon
Its humane splendor made me think *So what?*

One May noon in the Royal Park, among
The flora of l'Agneau Mystique—
Cypress, mimosa, laurel, palm—a Greek
Came up to name them for me in his tongue.

I thanked him; he thanked me, sat down. Peacocks
Trailed by, hard gray feet mashing overripe
But bitter oranges. I knew the type:
Superb, male, raucous, unclean, Orthodox

Ikon of appetite feathered to the eyes
With the electric blue of days that will
Not come again. My friend with time to kill
Asked me the price of cars in Paradise.

By which he meant my country, for in his
The stranger is a god in masquerade.
Failing to act that part, I am afraid
I was not human either—ah, who is?

He is, or was; had brothers and a wife;
Chauffeured a truck; last Friday broke his neck
Against a tree. We have no way to check
These headlong emigrations out of life.

Try, I suppose, we must, as even Valéry said,
And said more grandly than I ever shall—
Turning shut lids to the August sun, and all
Such neon figments (amber, green, and red)

Of incommunicable energy
As in my blindness wake, and at a blink
Vanish, and were the clearest hint, I think,
Of what I have been, am, and care to be.

3. CARNIVALS

Three good friends in as many months have complained,
"You were nice, James, before your trip. Or so
I thought. But you have changed. I know, I know,
People do change. Well, I'm surprised, I'm pained."

Before they disappeared into the night
Of what they said, I'd make a stab at mouthing
Promises that meant precisely nothing
And never saved my face. For they were right.

These weren't young friends, what's more. Youth would explain
Part of it. I have kept somewhere a page
Written at sixteen to myself at twice that age,
Whom I accuse of having become the vain

Flippant unfeeling monster I now am—
To hear them talk—and exhorting me to recall
Starlight on an evening in late fall
1943, and the walk with M,

To die in whose presence seemed the highest good.
I met M and his new wife last New Year's.
We rued the cold war's tainted atmospheres
From a corner table. It was understood

Our war was over. We had made our peace
With—everything. The heads of animals
Gazed in forbearance from the velvet walls.
Great drifts of damask cleaned our lips of grease.

Then L—her "Let's be friends" and her clear look
Returned in disbelief. I had a herd
Of *friends*. I wanted love, if love's the word
On the foxed spine of the long-mislaid book.

A thousand and one nights! They were grotesque.
Stripping the blubber from my catch, I lit
The oil-soaked wick, then could not see by it.
Mornings, a black film lay upon the desk

. . . Where just a week ago I thought to delve
For images of those years in a Plain Cover.
Some light verse happened as I looked them over:

Postcards from Hamburg, Circa 1912

The ocelot's yawn, a sepia-dim
Shamelessness from nun's coif to spike heels,
She strokes his handlebar who kneels
To do for her what a dwarf does for him.
The properties are grim,

Are, you might want to say, unsexed
By use. A divan covered with a rug,
A flat Methusalem of Krug
Appear from tableau to tableau. The next
Shows him with muscle flexed

In resurrection from his underwear,
Gaining an underworld to harrow.
He steers her ankles like—like a wheelbarrow.
The dwarf has slipped out for a breath of air,
Leaving the monstrous pair.

Who are they? What does their charade convey?
Maker and Muse? Demon and Doll?
"All manners are symbolic"—Hofmannsthal.
Here's the dwarf back with cronies . . . oh I *say!*
Forget about it. They,

In time, in pain, unlearned their tricks.
Only the shrouded focuser of the lens
May still be chasing specimens
From his lone bathysphere deep in the Styx.
St. Pauli's clock struck six;

Sighing, "The death of sin is wages,"
He paid his models, bade them dress and go,
Earthlings once more, incognito
Down swarming boulevards, the contagious-
ly easy, final stages,

Dodged even by the faithful, one of whom
(Morose Great-Uncle Alastair)
Brought back these effigies and would shortly bear
Their doctrine unconfessed, we may assume,
Into his brazen tomb.

We found the postcards after her divorce,
I and Aunt Alix. She turned red with shame,
Then white, then thoughtful. "Ah, they're all the same—
Men, I mean." A pause. "Not you, of course."

And then: "We'll burn them. Light the fire." I must
Meanwhile have tucked a few into my shirt.
I spent the night rekindling with expert
Fingers—but that phase needn't be discussed. . . .

"The soul, which in infancy could not be told from the body,
came with age to resemble *a body one no longer had*, whose trans-
ports went far beyond what passes, now, for sensation. All irony
aside, the libertine *was* 'in search of his soul'; nightly he labored
to regain those firelit lodgings. . . . Likewise, upon the Earth's
mature body we inflict a wealth of gross experience—drugs,
drills, bombardments—with what effect? A stale *frisson*, a waste
of resources all too analogous to our own. Natural calamities (tu-
mor and apoplexy no less than flood and volcano) may at last be
hailed as positive reassurances, perverse if you like, of life in the
old girl yet."

GERMAINE NAHMAN

". . . faced with such constant bickering, Cynthia would have to
pinch herself to recall how warmly and deeply those two did, in
fact, love one another."

A. H. CLARENDON, *Psyche's Sisters*

Love. Warmth. Fist of sunlight at last
Pounding emphatic on the gulf. High wails
From your white ship: The heart prevails!
Affirm it! Simple decency rides the blast!—
Phrases that, quick to smell blood, lurk like sharks
Within a style's transparent lights and darks.

The Thousand and Second Night

The lips part. The plume trembles. You're afloat
Upon the breathing, all-reflecting deep.
The past recedes and twinkles, falls asleep.
Fear is unworthy, say the stars by rote;
What destinations have been yours till now
Unworthy, says the leaping prow.

O skimmer of deep blue
Volumes fraught with rhyme and reason,
Once the phosphorescent meshes loosen
And the objects of your quest slip through,
Almost you can overlook a risen
Brow, a thin, black dawn on the horizon.

Except that in this virgin hemisphere
One city calls you—towers, drums, conches, bells
Tolling each year's more sumptuous farewells
To flesh. Among the dancers on the pier
Glides one figure in a suit of bones,
Whose savage grace alerts the chaperones.

He picks you out from thousands. He intends
Perhaps no mischief. Yet the dog-brown eyes
In the chalk face that stiffens as it dries
Pierce you with the eyes of those three friends.
The mask begins to melt upon your face.
A hush has fallen in the market place,

And now the long adventure

Let that wait.
I'm tired, it's late at night.

Tomorrow, if it is given me to conquer
An old distrust of imaginary scenes,
Scenes not lived through yet, the few final lines
Will lie on the page and the whole ride at anchor.

I'm home, of course. It's winter. Real
Snow fills the road. On the unmade
Brass bed lies my adored Scheherazade,
Eight-ninths asleep, tail twitching to the steel

Band of the steam heat's dissonant calypso.
The wind has died. Where would I be
If not here? There's so little left to see!
Lost friends, my long ago

Voyages, I bless you for sore
Limbs and mouth kissed, face bronzed and lined,
An earth held up, a text not wholly undermined
By fluent passages of metaphor.

4
Now if the class will turn back to this, er,
Poem's first section—Istanbul—I shall take
What little time is left today to make
Some brief points. So. The rough pentameter

Quatrains give way, you will observe, to three
Interpolations, prose as well as verse.
Does it come through how each in turn refers
To mind, body, and soul (or memory)?

It does? Good. No, I cannot say offhand
Why this should be. I find it vaguely satis—
Yes please? The poet quotes too much? Hm. That is
One way to put it. Mightn't he have planned

For his own modest effort to be seen
Against the yardstick of the "truly great"
(In Spender's phrase)? Fearing to overstate,
He lets *them* do it—lets their words, I mean,

Enhance his—Yes, what now? Ah. How and when
Did he "affirm"? Why, constantly. And how else
But in the form. Form's what affirms. That's well
Said, if I do—[*Bells ring.*] Go, gentlemen.

5

And when the long adventure reached its end,
I saw the Sultan in a glass, grown old,
While she, his fair wife still, her tales all told,
Smiled at him fondly. "O my dearest friend,"

Said she, "and lord and master from the first,
Release me now. Your servant would refresh
Her soul in that cold fountain which the flesh
Knows not. Grant this, for I am faint with thirst."

And he: "But it is I who am your slave.
Free me, I pray, to go in search of joys
Unembroidered by your high, soft voice,
Along that stony path the senses pave."

They wept, then tenderly embraced and went
Their ways. She and her fictions soon were one.
He slept through moonset, woke in blinding sun,
Too late to question what the tale had meant.

MAISIE

1

One morning I shall find
I have slept with your full weight upon my heart,
Your motors and my breathing reconciled.
The edges of the blind,

The crack beneath the door will have blanched with day,
The walls will be about to jar apart
And sun to dust my lids deep in the opened flower.
And still I shall not have sent you away.

2

When you came home without your sex
You hid in the cupboard under the sink.
Its gasps and gurglings must have helped somehow.

The second noon you ventured forth,
A silent star, furred up to tragic eyes,
Hazarding recognition in a restaurant.

It was horrible to see how much
You honestly cared about food and comfort.
The dishes refused! The chairs tried one by one!

Eunuch and favorite both,
You loll about, exuding that old magic
There is mercifully no longer a market for.

3

For the good of the guest who has not yet looked over
The roof garden's brink to the eaves just below,
You shudder there long enough only to shriek

(If eyes could shriek, and if they were ever
Eyes, those chalcedony bonfires): O
Scarpia! Avanti a Dio!
                    —then plummet from view,
Leaving the newcomer aghast and weak.

VIOLENT PASTORAL

Against a thunderhead's
Blue marble, the eagle
Mounts with the lamb in his clutch:
Two wings, four hooves,

One pulse pounding, pounding,
So little time being given
To feel the earth shrunken,
Gong-tilt of waters,

To be at once helplessly
Aching talon and bleating
Weight, both,
Lest the pact break,

To link the rut in dust
When the rope shortens
Between foreleg and stake
With the harder spiral of making

For a nest wrapped in lightnings
And quilted with their beaks who not yet,
As with their bones who no longer,
Are wholly brothers;

Beyond Arcadia at last,
Wing, hoof, one oriented creature,
Snake-scream of pride
And bowels of fright

Lost in the rainbow, to be one
Even with the shepherd
Still looking up, who understood
And was not turned to stone.

TIME

for B. V. Winebaum

Ever that Everest
Among concepts, as prize for fruitful
Grapplings with which
The solved crossword puzzle has now and then
Eclipsed Blake's "Sun-Flower"
(Not that one wanted a letter changed in either)
And jazz believed at seventeen
So parodied the slopes
That one mistook the mountain for a cloud . . .

Or there was blessed Patience:
Fifty-two chromosomes permitting
Trillions of "lives"—some few
Triumphant, the majority
Blocked, doomed, yet satisfying, too,
In that with each, before starting over,
You could inquire beneath
The snowfield, the vine-monogram, the pattern
Of winged cyclists, to where the flaw lay
Crocus-clean, a trail inching between
Sheer heights and drops, and reach what might have been.

All day you had meant
To write letters, turn the key
In certain friendships, be ticked through at dusk
By hard, white, absent faces.

Let's say you went
So far as to begin: "It's me! Forgive . . ."
Too late. From the alcove came his cough,
His whimper—the old man whom sunset wakes.
Truly, could you bear another night

105

Time

Keeping him company while he raved, agreeing
To Persia on horseback, just you two! when even
The garden path had been forbidden,
He was so feeble. Feeble!

He grasped your pulse in his big gray-haired hand,
Crevasses opening, numb azure. *Wait*
He breathed and glittered: *You'll regret*
You want to   Read my will first   Don't
Your old father   All he has   Be yours

Hours you raised the dark rum to his lips.
Your eyes burned. Your voice said:
"All right, we'll read Cervantes, we'll take trips.
She you loved lives. You'll see her in the morning.
You'll get well, you'll be proud of me. Don't smile!
I love you. I'll find work. You'll—I'll—"

It was light and late.
You could not remember
Sleeping. It hurt to rise.
There stood
Those features' ice-crowned, tanned—by what?—
Landmark, like yours, unwrinkled in repose.
Pouring tea strong and hot,
You swiftly wrote:

". . . this long silence. I don't know what's the matter with me.
All winter I have been trying to discipline myself—'Empty the
mind,' as they say in the handbooks, 'concentrate upon one
thing, any thing, the snowflake, the granite it falls upon, the
planet risen opposite, etc., etc.'—and failing, failing. Quick-
sands of leisure! Now summer's here, I *think*. Each morning a
fog rolls in from the sea. It would lift, perhaps, if you were to
come and speak to it. Will you? Do! One catches the ferry
at. . . ."

The pen reels from your hand. Were you asleep?
Who were you writing to? Annette? Me? Jake?
Later, smoothing the foothills of the sheet,
You take up your worn pack.

Above their gay crusaders' dress
The monarchs' mouths are pinched and bleak.
Staggering forth in ranks of less and less
Related cards, condemned to the mystique

Of a redeeming One,
An Ace to lead them home, sword, stave, and axe,
Power, Riches, Love, a place to lay them down
In dreamless heaps, the reds, the blacks,

Old Adams and gray Eves
Escort you still. Perhaps this time . . . ?
A Queen in the discarded suit of Leaves,
Earth dims and flattens as you climb

And heaven, darkened, steams
Upon the trembling disk of tea.
Sixty or seventy more games
And you can go the rest alone maybe—

Arriving then at something not unlike
Meaning relieved of sense,
To plant a flag there on that needle peak
Whose diamond grates in the revolving silence.

CHARLES ON FIRE

Another evening we sprawled about discussing
Appearances. And it was the consensus
That while uncommon physical good looks
Continued to launch one, as before, in life
(Among its vaporous eddies and false calms),
Still, as one of us said into his beard,
"Without your intellectual and spiritual
Values, man, you are sunk." No one but squared
The shoulders of his own unloveliness.
Long-suffering Charles, having cooked and served the meal,
Now brought out little tumblers finely etched
He filled with amber liquor and then passed.
"Say," said the same young man, "in Paris, France,
They do it this way"—bounding to his feet
And touching a lit match to our host's full glass.
A blue flame, gentle, beautiful, came, went
Above the surface. In a hush that fell
We heard the vessel crack. The contents drained
As who should step down from a crystal coach.
Steward of spirits, Charles's glistening hand
All at once gloved itself in eeriness.
The moment passed. He made two quick sweeps and
Was flesh again. "It couldn't matter less,"
He said, but with a shocked, unconscious glance
Into the mirror. Finding nothing changed,
He filled a fresh glass and sank down among us.

THE BROKEN HOME

Crossing the street,
I saw the parents and the child
At their window, gleaming like fruit
With evening's mild gold leaf.

In a room on the floor below,
Sunless, cooler—a brimming
Saucer of wax, marbly and dim—
I have lit what's left of my life.

I have thrown out yesterday's milk
And opened a book of maxims.
The flame quickens. The word stirs.

Tell me, tongue of fire,
That you and I are as real
At least as the people upstairs.

My father, who had flown in World War I,
Might have continued to invest his life
In cloud banks well above Wall Street and wife.
But the race was run below, and the point was to win.

Too late now, I make out in his blue gaze
(Through the smoked glass of being thirty-six)
The soul eclipsed by twin black pupils, sex
And business; time was money in those days.

Each thirteenth year he married. When he died
There were already several chilled wives
In sable orbit—rings, cars, permanent waves.
We'd felt him warming up for a green bride.

He could afford it. He was "in his prime"
At three score ten. But money was not time.

When my parents were younger this was a popular act:
A veiled woman would leap from an electric, wine-dark car
To the steps of no matter what—the Senate or the Ritz Bar—
And bodily, at newsreel speed, attack

No matter whom—Al Smith or José Maria Sert
Or Clemenceau—veins standing out on her throat
As she yelled *War mongerer! Pig! Give us the vote!*,
And would have to be hauled away in her hobble skirt.

What had the man done? Oh, made history.
Her business (he had implied) was giving birth,
Tending the house, mending the socks.

Always that same old story—
Father Time and Mother Earth,
A marriage on the rocks.

One afternoon, red, satyr-thighed
Michael, the Irish setter, head
Passionately lowered, led
The child I was to a shut door. Inside,

Blinds beat sun from the bed.
The green-gold room throbbed like a bruise.
Under a sheet, clad in taboos
Lay whom we sought, her hair undone, outspread,

And of a blackness found, if ever now, in old
Engravings where the acid bit.
I must have needed to touch it
Or the whiteness—was she dead?
Her eyes flew open, startled strange and cold.
The dog slumped to the floor. She reached for me. I fled.

Tonight they have stepped out onto the gravel.
The party is over. It's the fall
Of 1931. They love each other still.

She: Charlie, I can't stand the pace.
He: Come on, honey—why, you'll bury us all!

A lead soldier guards my windowsill:
Khaki rifle, uniform, and face.
Something in me grows heavy, silvery, pliable.

How intensely people used to feel!
Like metal poured at the close of a proletarian novel,
Refined and glowing from the crucible,
I see those two hearts, I'm afraid,
Still. Cool here in the graveyard of good and evil,
They are even so to be honored and obeyed.

. . . Obeyed, at least, inversely. Thus
I rarely buy a newspaper, or vote.
To do so, I have learned, is to invite
The tread of a stone guest within my house.

Shooting this rusted bolt, though, against him,
I trust I am no less time's child than some
Who on the heath impersonate Poor Tom
Or on the barricades risk life and limb.

Nor do I try to keep a garden, only
An avocado in a glass of water—
Roots pallid, gemmed with air. And later,

When the small gilt leaves have grown
Fleshy and green, I let them die, yes, yes,
And start another. I am earth's no less.

A child, a red dog roam the corridors,
Still, of the broken home. No sound. The brilliant
Rag runners halt before wide-open doors.
My old room! Its wallpaper—cream, medallioned
With pink and brown—brings back the first nightmares,
Long summer colds, and Emma, sepia-faced,
Perspiring over broth carried upstairs
Aswim with golden fats I could not taste.

The real house became a boarding school.
Under the ballroom ceiling's allegory
Someone at last may actually be allowed
To learn something; or, from my window, cool
With the unstiflement of the entire story,
Watch a red setter stretch and sink in cloud.

LITTLE FANFARE FOR
FELIX MAGOWAN

Up beyond sense and praise,
There at the highest trumpet blast
Of Fahrenheit, the sun is a great friend.
He is so brilliant and so warm!
Yet when his axle smokes and the spokes blaze
And he founders in dusk (or seems to),
Remember: he cannot change. It's earth, it's time,
Whose child you now are, quietly
Blotting him out. In the blue stare you raise
To your mother and father already the miniature,
Merciful, and lifelong eclipse,
Felix, has taken place;
The black pupil rimmed with rays
Contracted to its task—
That of revealing by obscuring
The sunlike friend behind it.
Unseen by you, may he shine back always
From what you see, from others. So welcome, friend.
Welcome to earth, time, others; to
These cool darks, of sense, of language,
Each at once thread and maze.
Finally welcome, if you like, to this
James your father's mother's father's younger son
Contrived with love for you
During your first days.

THE MAD SCENE

Again last night I dreamed the dream called Laundry.
In it, the sheets and towels of a life we were going to share,
The milk-stiff bibs, the shroud, each rag to be ever
Trampled or soiled, bled on or groped for blindly,
Came swooning out of an enormous willow hamper
Onto moon-marbly boards. We had just met. I watched
From outer darkness. I had dressed myself in clothes
Of a new fiber that never stains or wrinkles, never
Wears thin. The opera house sparkled with tiers
And tiers of eyes, like mine enlarged by belladonna,
Trained inward. There I saw the cloud-clot, gust by gust,
Form, and the lightning bite, and the roan mane unloosen.
Fingers were running in panic over the flute's nine gates.
Why did I flinch? I loved you. And in the downpour laughed
To have us wrung white, gnarled together, one
Topmost mordent of wisteria,
As the lean tree burst into grief.

A CARPET NOT BOUGHT

World at his feet,
Labor of generations—
No wonder the veins race.
In old Kazanjian's
Own words, "Love that carpet.
Forget the price."

Leaving the dealer's,
It was as if he had
Escaped quicksand. He
Climbed his front steps, head
High, full of dollars.
He poured the wife a brandy—

And that night not a blessed
Wink slept. The back yard
Lay senseless, bleak,
Profoundly scarred
By the moon's acid.
One after another clock

Struck midnight; one. Up through
His bare footsoles
Quicksilver shoots overcoming
The trellis of pulse
—Struck two, struck three—
Held him there, dreaming.

Kingdom reborn
In colors seen
By the hashish-eater—
Ice-pink, alizarin,
Pearl; maze shorn
Of depth; geometer

A Carpet Not Bought

To whom all desires
Down to the last silken
Wisp o' the will
Are known: what the falcon
Sees when he soars,
What wasp and oriole

Think when they build—
And all this could
Be bargained for! Lord,
Wasn't it time you stood
On grander ground than cold
Moon-splintered board?

Thus the admired
Artifact, like clock
Or snake, struck till its poison
Was gone. Day broke,
The fever with it. Merde!
Who wanted *things?* He'd won.

Flushed on the bed's
White, lay a figure whose
Richness he sensed
Dimly. It reached him as
A cave of crimson threads
Spun by her mother against

That morning in their life
When sons with shears
Should set the pattern free
To ripple air's long floors
And bear him safe
Over a small waved sea.

THE CURRENT

Down the dawn-brown
River the charcoal woman
Swept in a boat thin
As the old moon.
White tremblings darted and broke
Under her hat's crown.
A paddle-stroke
And she was gone, in her wake
Only miniature
Whirlpools, her faint
Ritualistic cries.

Now up the stream,
Urging an unwilling
Arc of melon rind
Painted red to match
His wares, appeared
The meat vendor.
The young, scarred face
Under the white brim
Glowed with strain
And flamelike ripplings.
He sat in a cloud of flies.

If, further on,
Someone was waiting to thread
Morsels of beef
Onto a green
Bamboo sliver
And pose the lean brochette
Above already glowing
Embers, the river,
Flowing in one direction
By moon, by sun,
Would not be going
To let it happen yet.

FROM THE CUPOLA

for H. M.

The sister who told fortunes prophesied
A love-letter. In the next mail it came.
You didn't recognize the writer's name
And wondered he knew yours. Ah well. That seed

Has since become a world of blossom and bark.
The letters fill a drawer, the gifts a room.
No hollow of your day is hidden from
His warm concern. Still you are in the dark.

Too much understanding petrifies.
The early letters struck you as blackmail.
You have them now by heart, a rosy veil
Colors the phrase repaired to with shut eyes.

Was the time always wrong for you to meet?—
Not that he ever once proposed as much.
Your sisters joke about it. "It's too rich!
Somebody Up There loves you, Psyche sweet."

Tell me about him, then. Not a believer,
I'll hold my tongue while you, my dear, dictate.
Him I have known too little (or, of late,
Too well) to trust my own view of your lover.

Oh but one has many, many tongues!
And you will need a certain smouldering five
Deep in the ash of something I survive,
Poke and rummage with as reluctant tongs

As possible. The point won't be to stage
One of our torchlit hunts for truth. Truth asks
Just this once to sleep with fiction, masks
Of tears and laughter on the moonstruck page;

118

To cauterize what babbles to be healed—
Just this once not by candor. Here and now,
Psyche, I quench that iron lest it outglow
A hovering radiance your fingers shield.

Renaissance features grafted onto Greek
Revival, glassed, hexagonal lookouts crown
Some of the finest houses in this town.
By day or night, cloud, sunbeam, lunatic streak,

They alternately ravish and disown
Earth, sky, and water—Are you with me? Speak.

SUNLIGHT   Crossfire
of rays and shadows each
glancing off a windowpane a stone
You alone my correspondent

have remained sheer
projection   Hurt   Not gravely   Not at all
Your bloodlessness a glaze
of thin thin varnish where I kneel

Were the warm drop
upon your letter oil and were that page
your sleeping person then
all would indeed be lost

Our town is small
its houses built like temples
The rare stranger I let pass with lowered
eyes   He also could be you

Nights the last red
wiped from my lips the harbor
blinking out gem by gem how utterly
we've been undressed

From the Cupola

You will not come
to the porch at noon will you rustling your wings
or masked as crone or youth
The mouths behind our faces kiss

Kindlings of truth
Risen from the dawn mist
some wriggling silver in a tern's beak scrawls
joyous memoranda onto things

TODAY I have your letter from the South
where as a child I   but of course you know
Three times I've read it at my attic window
A city named for palms half mummy and half myth
pools flashing talking birds the world of my
first vision of you Psyche   Though it's May

that could be frost upon the apple trees
silvery plump as sponges above the pale
arm of the Sound and the pane is chill to feel
I live now by the seasons burn and freeze
far from that world where nothing changed or died
unless to be reborn on the next tide

You daylong in the saddles of foaming opal
ride   I am glad   Come dusk lime juice and gin
deepen the sunset under your salt skin
I've tasted that side of the apple
A city named for palms half desert and half dream
its dry gold settles on my mouth   I bloom

Where nothing died.   Breaking on us like waves
the bougainvillea bloomed fell bloomed again
The new sea wall rose from the hurricane
and no less staunchly from the old freed slave's
ashes each night her grandchild climbed the stairs
to twitch white gauze across the stinging stars

City half dream half desert where at dawn
the sprinkler dervish whirled and all was crystalline
Within each house half brothel and half shrine
up from the mirror tabletop had flown
by noon the shadow of each plate each spoon to float
in light that warbled on the ceiling   Wait

ALICE has entered talking

Any mirage if seen from a remote stand
point is refreshing   Yes but dust and heat
lie at its heart   Poor Psyche you forget
That was a cruel impossible wonderland

The very sidewalks suffered   Ours that used
to lead can you remember to the beach
I felt it knew and waited for us each
morning to trot its length in teardrop punctured shoes

when in fact the poor dumb thing lay I now know
under a dark spell cast from quite another
quarter the shadow of a towering mother
smooth as stone and thousandbreasted though

her milk was watery scant so much for love
false like everything in that whole world
However   This shadow that a royal palm hurled
onto the sidewalk from ten yards above

day night rustling and wrestling never shattered
except to mend back forth or lost its grip
the batwing offspring of her ladyship
Our orchid stucco house looked on greenshuttered

stoic   But the sidewalk suffered most
Like somebody I shall not name it lacked
perspective   It failed absolutely to detect
the root of all that evil   The clues it missed

From the Cupola

Nights after a windstorm great yellow paper
dry branches lying on the curb in heaps
like fancy dress don't ask me whose someone who steps
forth and is changed by the harsh moonlight to vapor

the sidewalk could only grit itself and shift
Some mornings respite   A grisaille opaque
as poured concrete   And yet by ten o'clock
the phantom struck again in a first sunshaft

Off to the beach   Us nurse in single file
Those days we'd meet our neighbor veiled and hatted
tanagra leading home out of the sun she hated
a little boy with water wings   We'd smile

then hold our breaths to pass a barricade
of black smells rippling up from the soft hot
brink of the mirage past which sidewalks could not
follow   Ours stood there crumbling then obeyed

a whisper back of it and turned   The sea the loose
unshadowed sand too free white heterodox
ever to be congealed into sidewalks
ours never saw   GIVE ME THE SNAPPED SHOELACE

LIZARDS ANTS SCRAPS OF SILVER FOIL
hoarse green tongues begged from each new crack   No use
The shadow trod it as our nightmares us
Then we moved here where gray skies are the rule

What   Why not simply have cut down the tree
Psyche I can't believe my   Hush   You child
Cut down the   I've got gooseflesh   Feel   I'm chilled
My sister's hyperthyroid eyes fix me

The whites lackluster shot with miniature
red brambles abruptly glitter overspill
down powdered cheeks   Alice can weep at will
How to convey the things I feel for her

122

She is more strange than Iceland bathed all night
an invalid in sunshine   Lava cliffs
The geyser that erupts the loon that laughs
I move to kiss her but she hums a note

and licks her lips   *Well darling I must fly*
before you read what it does not intend
about yourself and your mysterious friend
say or some weird rivalry that I

may once have harbored though I harbor none
now nor does Gertrude not the tiniest pang
into this long but kindly meant harangue
She nods and leaves the room   And I am here alone

I place the ladder hoist from rung to rung
my pail and cloths into a cupola glassed
entirely with panes some tinted amethyst
it is my task to clean   Up here among

spatterings and reflections wipe as I will
these six horizons still the rain's dry ghost
and my own features haunt the roofs the coast
How does one get to know a landscape well

When did we leave the South   Why do we live indoors
I wonder sweating to the cadence   Even
on sunless days the cupola is an oven
Views blur   This thing we see them through endures

MIDNIGHT   I dream I dream   The slow moon eludes
one stilled cloud   Din of shimmerings   From across the Sound
what may have begun as no more
than a willow's sleepwalking outline quickens detaches
comes to itself in the cupola
panics from pane to pane and then impulsively
surrendering fluttering by now the sixteenfold
wings of the cherubim unclipped by faith or reason

From the Cupola

stands there my dream made whole
over whose walls again
a red vine black in moonlight crawls
made habitable   Each cell of the concrete
fills with sweet light   The wave breaks
into tears   Come if it's you   Step down
to where I   Stop   For at your touch the dream

cracks the angel tenses flees

NOON finds me faced by a small troop of furies
They are my senses shrill and ominous
We who were trained they cry *to do your pleasure*
are kept like children   Is this fair to us

Dear ones I say bending to kiss their faces
trust me   One day you'll understand   Meanwhile
suppose we think of things to raise our spirits
and leading the two easiest to beguile

into the kitchen feed them shots of Bourbon
Their brother who loves Brahms conceives a wish
for gems from L'Africana played at volumes
that make the dwarf palm shudder in its dish

The pale one with your eyes restively flashing
takes in the dock the ashen Sound the sky
The fingers of the eldest brush my features
But you are smiling she says coldly   *Why*

    STAR or candle being lit
        but to shed itself
    into blackness partly night's
sure that no less golden warm than it
        is our love
    will have missed the truth by half
    We see according to our lights

Eros   husband   names distort
      you who have no name
Peace upon your neophytes
Help me when the christenings shall start
         o my love
    to defend your sleep from them
    and see according to our lights

Ah and should discernment's twin
      tyrants adamant
    for their meal of pinks and whites
be who call those various torches in
       help me love
    This is nothing I shall want
    We see according to our lights

When as written you have lapsed
      back into the god
    darts and wings and appetites
what of him the lover all eclipsed
       by sheer love
    Shut my eyes it does no good
    Who will ever put to rights

Psyche, hush. This is me, James,
      Writing lest he think
Of the reasons why he writes—
    Boredom, fear, mixed vanities and shames;
       Also love.
    From my phosphorescent ink
    Trickle faint unworldly lights

Down your face. Come, we'll both rest.
      Weeping? You must not.
All our pyrotechnic flights
Miss the sleeper in the pitch-dark breast.
      He is love:
    He is everyone's blind spot.
    We see according to our lights.

"What's that sound? Is it you, dear?"
"Yes. I was just eating something."
"What?"
"I don't know—I mean, an apricot . . ."
"Hadn't you best switch on the light and make sure?"
"No, thank you, Gertrude."
A hurt silence ensued.

"Oh, Psyche!" her sister burst out at length. "Here you are, surrounded by loving kin, in a house crammed with lovely old things, and what do you crave but the unfamiliar, the 'transcendental'? I declare, you're turning into the classic New England old maid!"

  . . . .

Psyche's hands dropped from her wet, white face. The time had come—except that Time, like Love, wears a mask in this story, whose action requires perhaps thirty-six hours of Spring, perhaps thirty-six Springs of a life—a moment nevertheless had come to take the electric torch and leave her sisters without a word. Later she was to recall a tear-streaked muzzle, the marvelous lashed golds of an iris reflecting her own person backed by ever tinier worlds of moonlight and tossing palms, then, at the center, blackness, a fixed point, a spindle on which everything had begun to turn. Piercing her to the brain.

Spelt out in brutal prose, all had been plain.

RAIN   Evening   The drive in   My sisters' gold sedan's
    eyes have gone dim and dark   windows are sealed
        For vision's sake two wipers wield
    the automatic coquetry of fans

In the next car young Eros and his sweetheart sit
    fire and saltwater still from their embrace
        Grief plays upon his sated face
    Her mask of tears does not exactly fit

The love goddess his mother overflows a screen
    sixty feet wide or seems to   Who can plumb
        those motes of rose and platinum
    At once they melt back into the machine

throbbing dry and dispassionate beyond our ken
    to spool her home whose beauty flabbergasts
        The nervous systems of her guests
    drink and drink the sparkling staleness in

Now in her element steam she looms up from a bath
    The hero's breastplate mirrors her red lips
        It burns and clouds   As waterdrops
    course down the monumental cheeks of both

they kiss   My sisters turn on me from either side
    shrieking with glee under the rainlight mask
        fondle and pinch in mean burlesque
    of things my angel you and I once tried

In no time he alone is left of a proud corps
    That dustcloud hides triumphant fleeing Huns
        Lips parched by a montage of suns
    he cannot taste our latter night's downpour

while she by now my sisters fatten upon fact
    is on location in Djakarta where
        tomorrow's sun illumines her
    emoting in strange arms   It's all an act

Eros are you like her so false a naked glance
    turns you into that slackjawed fleshproud youth
        driving away   Was he your truth
    Is it too late to study ignorance

These fictive lives these loves of the comedian
    so like so unlike ours which hurt and heal
        are what the gods know   You can feel
    lust and fulfillment Eros no more than

ocean its salt depths or uranium its hot
    disintegrative force or I our fable
        My interest like the rain grown feeble
    a film of sorrow on my eyes they shut

I may already be part god   Asleep awake
    some afterglow as of a buried heaven
        keeps flickering through me   I may even
    learn to love it Eros for your sake

MORNING   The task is done   When my sisters wake
they will look once more upon pale water and clear sky
a fair far brow of land
with its fillet of Greek trees oak apple willow
and here below in the foreground
across a street finished down to the last detail
a red clapboard temple   The neat outlines
it's a warehouse really have been filled with colors
dull red flaking walls   white trim
and pediment   tar roof patched black on black
Greek colors   An effect I hope
not too much spoiled by a big yellow legend
BOAT WORKS on the roof which seagulls helicopters
the highup living and the happy dead
are in a position to read
Outside indeed a boat lies covered with tarpaulin
Old headlines mend a missing pane   The warehouse
seems but in the time it takes to say *abandoned*
a face male old molepale in sun
though blinded by the mullion's shadow
has floated to an eerie scale the rising
wind flutes out of the oaken depths
I look away   When I look back
the panic's over   It is afternoon
Now the window reflects my sisters' white
mock Ionic portico and me emerging
blinking   Too bright to bear or turn from

spring's first real sun burns on the numb blue Sound
Beyond the warehouse past the round GULF sign
whose warning it ignores a baby dock has waded
The small waves stretch their necks gulls veer and scold
I walk the length of our Greek Revival village
from library to old blind lighthouse
Like one entranced who talks as awake she cannot
a potpourri of dead chalkpetal dialects
dead anyhow all winter
lips caulked with faded pollen and dust of cloves
I find that I can break the cipher
come to light along certain humming branches
make out not only *apple blossom* and *sun*
but perfectly the dance of darker undertones
on pavement or white wall   It is this dance I know
that cracks the pavement   I do know
Finally I reach a garden where I am to uproot
the last parsnips for my sisters' dinner
Not parsnips mastodons   But this year's greens
already frill them and they pull easily
from the soft ground   Two of the finest
are tightly interlocked have grown that way   They lie
united in the grave of sunny air
as in their breathing living dark
I look at them a long while
mealy and soiled in one another's arms
and blind full to the ivory marrow
with tender blindness   Then I bury them
once more in memory of us
Back home   Gold skies   My basket full
Lifting it indoors I turn   The little dock
It is out there still on stilts in freezing water
It must know by now
that no one is coming after it that it must wait
for morning for next week for summer
by which time it will have silvered and splintered
and the whitewinged boats and the bridegroom's burning sandals
will come too late   It's dark   It's dinner time

From the Cupola

Light the lamp my sisters call from where they eat
There follows a hushed preening and straining
wallpaper horsehair glass wood pewter glue
Now is their moment when all else goes black
and what is there but substance to turn to
Sister the lamp   The round
moon mallet has risen and struck   Of the warehouse pulverized
one faintest blueprint glimmers by which to build it
on the same spot tomorrow somehow right
Light your lamp Psyche dear
My hand is on the switch   I have done this
faithfully each night since the first
Tonight I think will not be different
Then soft light lights the room the furniture
a blush invades even the dropped lid
yes and I am here alone
I and my flesh and blood

Thank you, Psyche. I should think those panes
Were just about as clear as they can be.
It's time I turned my light on. Child, leave me.
Here on the earth we loved alone remains

One shrunken amphitheatre, look, to moon
Hugely above. Ranked glintings from within
Hint that a small articulate crowd has been
Gathered for days now, waiting. None too soon,

Whether in lower or in upper case,
Will come the Moment for the metal of each
To sally forth—once more into the breach!
Beyond it, glory lies, a virgin space

Acrackle in white hunger for the word.
We've seen what comes next. There is no pure deed.
A black-and-red enchanter, a deep-dyed
Coil of—No matter. One falls back, soiled, blurred.

And on the page, of course, black only. Damned
If I don't tire of the dark view of things.
I think of your "Greek colors" and it rings
A sweet bell. Time to live! Haven't I dimmed

That portion of the ribbon—whose red glows
Bright with disuse—sufficiently for a bit?
Tomorrow mayn't I start to pay my debt,
In wine, in heart's blood, to la vie en rose?

This evening it will do to be alone,
Here, with your girlish figures: parsnip, Eros,
Shadow, blossom, windowpane. The warehouse.
The lamp I smell in every other line.

Do you smell mine? From its rubbed brass a moth
Hurtles in motes and tatters of itself
—Be careful, tiny sister, drabbest sylph!—
Against the hot glare, the consuming myth,

Drops, and is still. My hands move. An intense,
Slow-paced, erratic dance goes on below.
I have received from whom I do not know
These letters. Show me, light, if they make sense.

DAYS OF 1964

Houses, an embassy, the hospital,
Our neighborhood sun-cured if trembling still
In pools of the night's rain . . .
Across the street that led to the center of town
A steep hill kept one company part way
Or could be climbed in twenty minutes
For some literally breathtaking views,
Framed by umbrella pines, of city and sea.
Underfoot, cyclamen, autumn crocus grew
Spangled as with fine sweat among the relics
Of good times had by all. If not Olympus,
An out-of-earshot, year-round hillside revel.

I brought home flowers from my climbs.
Kyria Kleo who cleaned for us
Put them in water, sighing *Virgin, Virgin*.
Her legs hurt. She wore brown, was fat, past fifty,
And looked like a Palmyra matron
Copied in lard and horsehair. How she loved
You, me, loved us all, the bird, the cat!
I think now she *was* love. She sighed and glistened
All day with it, or pain, or both.
(We did not notably communicate.)
She lived nearby with her pious mother
And wastrel son. She called me her real son.

I paid her generously, I dare say.
Love makes one generous. Look at us. We'd known
Each other so briefly that instead of sleeping
We lay whole nights, open, in the lamplight,
And gazed, or traded stories.

One hour comes back—you gasping in my arms
With love, or laughter, or both,
I having just remembered and told you
What I'd looked up to see on my way downtown at noon:

Poor old Kleo, her aching legs,
Trudging into the pines. I called,
Called three times before she turned.
Above a tight, skyblue sweater, her face
Was painted. Yes. Her face was painted
Clown-white, white of the moon by daylight,
Lidded with pearl, mouth a poinsettia leaf,
Eat me, pay me—the erotic mask
Worn the world over by illusion
To weddings of itself and simple need.

Startled mute, we had stared—was love illusion?—
And gone our ways. Next, I was crossing a square
In which a moveable outdoor market's
Vegetables, chickens, pottery kept materializing
Through a dream-press of hagglers each at heart
Leery lest he be taken, plucked,
The bird, the flower of that November mildness,
Self lost up soft clay paths, or found, foothold,
Where the bud throbs awake
The better to be nipped, self on its knees in mud—
Here I stopped cold, for both our sakes;

And calmer on my way home bought us fruit.

Forgive me if you read this. (And may Kyria Kleo,
Should someone ever put it into Greek
And read it aloud to her, forgive me, too.)
I had gone so long without loving,
I hardly knew what I was thinking.

Where I hid my face, your touch, quick, merciful,
Blindfolded me. A god breathed from my lips.
If that was illusion, I wanted it to last long;
To dwell, for its daily pittance, with us there,
Cleaning and watering, sighing with love or pain.
I hoped it would climb when it needed to the heights

133

Even of degradation, as I for one
Seemed, those days, to be always climbing
Into a world of wild
Flowers, feasting, tears—or was I falling, legs
Buckling, heights, depths,
Into a pool of each night's rain?
But you were everywhere beside me, masked,
As who was not, in laughter, pain, and love.

From The Fire Screen (1969)

LORELEI

The stones of kin and friend
Stretch off into a trembling, sweatlike haze.

They may not after all be stepping-stones
But you have followed them. Each strands you, then

Does not. Not yet. Not here.
Is it a crossing? Is there no way back?

Soft gleams lap the base of the one behind you
On which a black girl sings and combs her hair.

It's she who some day (when your stone is in place)
Will see that much further into the golden vagueness

Forever about to clear. Love with his chisel
Deepens the lines begun upon your face.

THE FRIEND OF THE FOURTH
DECADE

When I returned with drinks and nuts my friend
Had moved to the window seat, back to the view.

The clear central pane around which ran
Smaller ones stained yellow, crimson, blue,

Framed our country's madly whipping flag,
Its white pole above roofs, the sea beyond.

That it was time for the flag to be lowered shed
Light on my friend's tactful disinvolvement—

Or did he feel as chastening somehow
Those angry little stripes upon his shoulders?

A huge red sun flowed positively through
Him in spots, glazing, obscuring his person

To that of Anyman with ears aglow,
On a black cushion, gazing inward, mute.

After dinner he said, "I'm tired of understanding
The light in people's eyes, the smells, the food.

(By the way, those veal birds were delicious.
They're out of Fannie Farmer? I thought so.)

Tired of understanding what I hear,
The tones, the overtones; of knowing

Just what clammy twitchings thrive
Under such cold flat stones

As We-are-profoundly-honored-to-have-with-us
Or This-street-has-been-torn-up-for-your-convenience.

As for what I catch myself saying,
Don't believe me! I *despise* Thoreau.

I mean to learn, in the language of where I am going,
Barely enough to ask for food and love.

Listen," he went on. "I have this friend—
What's that face for? Did you think I had only one?

You are my oldest friend, remember. Well:
Karlheinrich collects stamps. I now spend mornings

With a bowl of water and my postcard box.
Cards from all over. God! Those were the years

I never used to throw out anything.
Each card then soaks five minutes while its ink

Turns to exactly the slow formal swirls
Through which a phoenix flies on Chinese silk.

These leave the water darker but still clear,
The text unreadable. It's true!

Cards from my mother, my great-uncle, you!
And the used waters deepen the sea's blue.

I cannot tell you what this does to me.
Scene upon scene's immersion and emergence

Rinsed of the word. The Golden Gate, Moroccan
Dancing boys, the Alps from Interlaken,

The Friend of the Fourth Decade

Fuji, the Andes, Titian's Venus, two
Mandrills from the Cincinnati zoo—

All *that* survives the flood, as does a lighter
Heart than I have had in many a day.

Salt lick big as a fist, heart, hoard
Of self one grew up prizing above rubies—

To feel it even by a grain dissolved,
Absolved I mean, recipient with writer,

By water holy from the tap, by air that dries,
Of having cared and having ceased to care . . ."

I nodded and listened, envious. When my friend
Had gone where he was going, I tried it, too.

The stamp slid off, of course, and the ink woke.
I watched my mother's *Dearest Son* unfurl

In blue ornate brief plungings-up:
Almost a wild iris taking shape.

I heard oblivion's thin siren singing,
And bore it bravely. At the hour's end

I had my answer. Chances are it was
Some simple matter of what ink she used,

And yet her message remained legible,
The memories it stirred did not elude me.

I put my postcards back upon the shelf.
Certain things die only with oneself.

"You should see Muhammed's taxi," wrote my friend.
"Pure junkyard Bauhaus, angular, dented white,

It trails a wedding veil of squawking dust.
Each ride is worth your life—except I'm just

Not afraid. I'm not.
Those chiefly who discern us have the juju

To take our lives. Bouncing beside Muhammed,
I smile and smoke, am indestructible.

Or else I just can't picture dying
On foreign soil. These years are years of grace.

The way I feel towards home is . . . dim.
Don't worry, I'll go back. Honeymoons end.

Nor does the just man cheat his native earth
Of its inalienable right to cover him."

Finally a dung-and-emerald oasis,
No place I knew of. "Here," he wrote on the back,

"Individual and type are one.
Do as I please, I *am* the simpleton

Whose last exploit is to have been exploited
Neck and crop. In the usual bazaar,

Darker, more crisscrossed than a beggar's palm,
Smell of money draws them after me,

I answer to whatever name they call,
Drink the sweet black condescending dregs,

Try on their hungers like a shirt of flame
(Well, a sports shirt of flame) whereby I've been

Picked clean, reborn each day increasingly
Conspicuous, increasingly unseen."

Behind a door marked DANGER
(This is a dream I have about my friend)

Swaddlings of his whole civilization,
Prayers, accounts, long priceless scroll,

Whip, hawk, prow, queen, down to some last
Lost comedy, all that fine writing

Rigid with rains and suns,
Are being gingerly unwound.

There. Now the mirror. Feel the patient's heart
Pounding—oh please, this once—

Till nothing moves but to a drum.
See his eyes darken in bewilderment—

No, in joy—and his lips part
To greet the perfect stranger.

16.ix.65

for Vassíli and Mimí

Summer's last half moon waning high
Dims and curdles. Up before the bees
On our friend's birthday, we have left him
To wake in their floating maze.

Light downward strokes of yellow, green, and rust
Render the almond grove. Trunk after trunk
Tries to get right, in charcoal,
The donkey's artless contrapposto.

Sunrise. On the beach
Two turkey gentlemen, heads shaven blue
Above dry silk kimonos sashed with swords,
Treat us to a Kabuki interlude.

The tiny fish risen excitedly
Through absolute transparence
Lie in the boat, gasping and fanning themselves
As if the day were warmer than the sea.

Cut up for bait, our deadest ones
Reappear live, by magic, on the hook.
Never anything big or gaudy—
Line after spangled line of light, light verse.

A radio is playing "Mack the Knife".
The morning's catch fills one straw hat.
Years since I'd fished. Who knows when in this life
Another chance will come?

Between our toes unused to sandals
Each step home strikes its match.
And now, with evening's four and twenty candles
Lit among stars, waves, pines

16.ix.65

To animate our friend's face, all our faces
About a round, sweet loaf,
Mavríli brays. We take him some,
Return with honey on our drunken feet.

WORDS FOR MARIA

Unjeweled in black as ever comedienne
Of mourning if not silent star of chic,
You drift, September nightwind at your back,
The half block from your flat to the Bon Goût,
Collapse, order a black
Espresso and my ouzo in that Greek
Reserved for waiters, crane to see who's who
Without removing your dark glasses, then,
Too audibly: "Eh, Jimmy, qui sont ces deux strange men?"

Curiosity long since killed the cat
Inside you. Sweet good nature, lack of guile,
These are your self-admitted foibles, no?
My countrymen, the pair in question, get
Up, glance our way, and go,
And we agree it will not be worthwhile
To think of funny nicknames for them yet,
Such as Le Turc, The Missing Diplomat,
Justine, The Nun, The Nut—ah now, speaking of that,

I'm calling *you* henceforth The Lunatic.
Today at 4 a.m. in a snack bar
You were discovered eating, if you please,
Fried squid; alone. Aleko stood aghast.
"Sit down, try some of these,"
You said and gave your shrug, as when, the car
Door shutting on your thumb, a faint sigh passed
Uninterpreted till Frederick
At table glimpsed your bloodstained Kleenex and was sick.

Sapphó has been to your new flat, she *says*.
Tony, who staggered there with the Empire
Mirror you wanted from his shop, tells how
You had him prop it in a chair and leave
That instant. Really now!
Let's plan a tiny housewarming. "My dear,

Impossible with L'Éternel Convive."
Tall, gleaming, it could sit for years, I guess,
Drinking the cool black teas of your appearances.

Not that you're much at home this season. By
Ten you are being driven to the shore—
A madness known as Maria's Gardening Phase.
I went along once, watched you prune, transplant,
Nails ragged, in a daze
Of bliss. A whitewashed cube with tout confort
You'd built but would not furnish. "Bah, one can't
Spend day and night in Eden. Chairs, beds—why?
Dormir, d'ailleurs, this far from the Bon Goût? I'd die!"

In smarter weeds than Eve's (Chanel, last year's)
You kneel to beds of color and young vines.
The chauffeur lounges smoking in the shade . . .
Before you know it, sunset. Brass-white, pink-
Blue wallowings. Dismayed
You recollect a world in which one dines,
Plays cards, endures old ladies, has to think.
The motor roars. You've locked up trowel and shears.
The whole revived small headland lurches, disappears

To float pale black all night against the sea,
A past your jasmines for the present grow
Dizzyingly from. About what went before
Or lies beneath, how little can one glean.
Girlhood, marriage, the war . . .
I'd like once (not now, here comes Giulio)
Really to hear—I mean—I didn't mean—
You paint a smiling mouth to answer me:
"Since when does L'Enfant care for archaeology?"

"Some people are not charmed. I'm among those,"
Sapphó said, livid. "Fond of one? Pure myth.
Fond of her chauffeur—period. I refuse
Flatly to see her." As for me, I've come

146

To take you for the muse
Of my off-days, and tell you so herewith
If only to make you smile, shrug, run a comb
Through foam-grayed hair the wind from Egypt blows
Across a brow of faint lines powdered tuberose.

KOSTAS TYMPAKIANÁKIS

Sit, friend. We'll be drinking and I'll tell you why.
Today I went to Customs to identify
My brother—it was him, all right, in spite of both
Feet missing from beneath his Army overcoat.

He was a handsome devil twice the size of me.
We're all good-looking in my family.
If you saw that brother, or what's left of him,
You'd understand at once the kind of man he'd been.

I have other brothers, one whose face I broke
In a family quarrel, and that's no joke:
I'm small but strong, when I get mad I fight.
Seven hundred vines of his were mine by right

And still are—fine! He's welcome to them.
I'm twenty-two. It's someone else's turn to dream.
I liked our school and teacher till they made me stop
And earn my living in a welder's shop.

Cousins and friends were learning jokes and games
At the Kafeneíon behind steamed-up panes.
I worked without a mask in a cold rain of sparks
That fell on you and burned—look, you can still see marks.

The German officer stubbed his *puro* out
On my mother's nipples but her mouth stayed shut.
She lived to bear me with one foot in the grave
And they never found my father in his mountain cave.

He died last year at eighty. To his funeral
Came a NATO Captain and an English General.
Our name is known around Herákleion
In all the hill towns, just ask anyone.

Outside our village up above Knossós
A railed-in plot of cypresses belongs to us,
Where we'll put my brother, and if there's room
One day I'll lie beside him till the crack of doom.

But I'd rather travel to a far-off land,
Though I never shall, and settle, do you understand?
The trouble here is not with sun and soil
So much as meanness in the human soul.

I worked a time in Germany, I saw a whore
Smile at me from inside her little lighted door.
She didn't want my money, she was kind and clean
With mirrors we submerged in like a submarine.

The girl I loved left me for a Rhodiot.
I should be broken-hearted but it's strange, I'm not.
Take me with you when you sail next week,
You'll see a different cosmos through the eyes of a Greek.

Or write my story down for people. Use my name.
And may it bring you all the wealth and fame
It hasn't brought its bearer. Here, let's drink our wine!
Who could have imagined such a life as mine?

OUZO FOR ROBIN

Dread of an impending umptieth
Birthday thinning blood to water, clear
Spirits to this opal-tinted white—
Uncle, the confusion unto death!

Last night's hurled glass. On the wall a mark
Explored by sunlight inching blindly
Forth from the tavern onto tree-tarred
Heights of gilt and moleskin, now gone dark.

Thorn needle launched in spinning grooves' loud
Black. A salt spray, a drenching music.
Each dance done, wet hawklike features cling
To one more tumblerful of numb cloud.

Joy as part of dread, rancor as part.
Lamplit swaying rafters. Later, stars.
Case presented, point by brilliant point,
Against the uncounselable heart.

Ground trampled hard. Again. The treasure
Buried. Rancor. Joy. Tonight's blank grin.
Threshold where the woken cherub shrieks
To stop it, stamping with displeasure.

TO MY GREEK

Dear nut
Uncrackable by nuance or debate,
Eat with your fingers, wear your bloomers to bed,

Under my skin stay nude. Let past and future

Perish upon our lips, ocean inherit
Those paper millions. Let there be no word
For justice, grief, convention; *you* be convention—
Goods, bads, kaló-kakó, cockatoo-raucous

Coastline of white printless coves

Already strewn with offbeat echolalia.
Forbidden Salt Kiss Wardrobe Foot Cloud Peach
—Name it, my chin drips sugar. Radiant dumbbell, each

Noon's menus and smalltalk leave you

Likelier, each sunset yawned away,
Hair in eyes, head bent above the strummed
Lexicon, gets by heart about to fail
This or that novel mode of being together

Without conjunctions. Still

I fear for us. Nights fall
We toss through blindly, drenched in her appraising
Glare, the sibyl I turn to

When all else fails me, when you do—

The mother tongue!
Her least slip a mirror triptych glosses,
Her automation and my mind are one.
Ancient in fishscale silver-blue,

To My Greek

What can she make of you? Her cocktail sweats

With reason: speech will rise from it,
Quite beyond your comprehension rise
Like blood to a slapped face, stingingly apt

If unrepeatable, tones one forgets

Even as one is changed for life by them,
Veins branching a cold coral,
Common sense veering into common scenes,
Tears, incoherent artifice,

Altar upset, cut glass and opaline

Schools ricocheting through the loud cave
Where lie my Latin's rusted treasure,
The bones, picked clean, of my Italian,

Where some blue morning also she may damn

Well find her windpipe slit with that same rainbow
Edge a mere weekend with you gives
To books, to living (anything to forego
That final drunken prophecy whereby,

Lacking her blessing, you my siren grow

Stout, serviceable, gray.
A fishwife shawled in fourth-hand idiom
Spouting my views to earth and heaven) —Oh,

Having chosen the way of little knowledge,

Trusted each to use the other
Kindly except in moments of gross need,
Come put the verb-wheel down
And kiss my mouth despite the foot in it.

Let schoolboys brave her shallows. Sheer

Lilting azure float them well above
Those depths the surfacer
Lives, when he does, alone to sound and sound.

The barest word be what I say in you.

NIKE

The lie shone in her face before she spoke it.
Moon-battered, cloud-torn peaks, mills, multitudes
Implied. A floating sphere
Her casuist had at most to suck his pen,
Write of *Unrivalled by truth's own*
For it to dawn upon me. Near the gate
A lone iris was panting, purple-tongued.
I thought of my village, of tonight's *Nabucco*
She would attend, according to the lie,
Bemedalled at the royal right elbow. High
Already on entr'acte kümmel, hearing as always
Through her ears the sad waltz of the slaves,
I held my breath in pity for the lie
Which nobody would believe unless I did.
Mines (unexploded from the last one) lent
Drama to its rainbow surface tension.
Noon struck. Far off, a cataract's white thread
Kept measuring the slow drop into the gorge.
I thought of his forge and crutch who hobbled
At her prayer earthward. What he touched bloomed.
Fire-golds, oil-blacks. The pond people
Seemed victims rather, bobbing belly-up,
Of constitutional vulnerability
Than dynamite colluding with a fast buck.
Everywhere soldiers were falling, reassembling,
As we unpacked our picnic, she and I.
No wiser than the ant. Prepared to die
For all we knew. And even at the end,
Faced with a transcript bound in sunset
Of muffled depositions underground,
She offered wine and cookies first. She asked,
Before the eyes were bandaged, the bubble burst
And what she uttered with what I held back
Ran in red spittle down the chin,
Asked why I could not have lived the lie.

Flicking a crumb off, diffident, asked why
I thought my loved ones had been left to dream
Whole nights unbridled in the bed's brass jail
Beneath a ceiling washed by her reflected snows.

LAST WORDS

My life, your light green eyes
Have lit on me with joy.
There's nothing I don't know
Or shall not know again,
Over and over again.
It's noon, it's dawn, it's night,
I am the dog that dies
In the deep street of Troy
Tomorrow, long ago —
Part of me dims with pain,
Becomes the stinging flies,
The bent head of the boy.
Part looks into your light
And lives to tell you so.

DAVID'S NIGHT IN VELIÈS

Into the flame Godmother put her hand,
Lulling the olive boughs.
Lymph welled from them. I too in her strange house
Kindled and smoked and did not understand.

Followed the Cyclopean meal:
Loaves, rice, hens, goats, gallons of sweet red wine.
I mellowed with the men
Who now waxed crackling, philosophical

—For all I knew—but then
Were on their feet, with flashlights, tramping out
In ancient Air Force overcoats
After the small birds roosting roundabout.

Chains glowing strong
Had bound me to her hearth. Photograph time!
A whole boxful explained in pantomime,
One by one. The string

Retied, warm-hearted questioning
Could start, in mime, about my life.
Each offhand white lie gladdened her, good queen
In whose domain the rueful

Dream was fact. Subdued
Came back her hunters. The lone ortolan,
Head lolling from a sideboard out of Oudry,
Would be my very own to breakfast on.

Bedtime. Inconceivable upper room
Ashiver in lamplight.
Bed clean as ice, heavy as ice
Its layers of coarsely woven pink and white

David's Night in Veliès

Woken at once to struggle out from. Bitter
Closet reeking welcome. Wind, moon, frost.
Piebald hindquarters of another guest.
Fowl's nervous titter.

Relieved of wine's last warmth, to lie and freeze . . .
Day would break, never fear;
Rime-sparkling courtesies melt into blue air
Like dew. One hour more? Two? Goodbye! Write please!

The road would climb in bracelets toward the pass,
The sun be high but low,
Each olive tree shed its white thawing shadow
On sallow grass,

Myself become the stranger who remembers
Fire, cold, a smile, a smell,
One tiny plucked form on the embers,
Slow claw raised in blessing or farewell.

ANOTHER AUGUST

Pines. The white, ochre-pocked houses. Sky unflawed. Upon so
much former strangeness a calm settles, glaze of custom to be
neither shattered nor shattered by. Home. Home at last.

Years past—blind, tattering
wind, hail, tears—my head was in those clouds
that now are dark pearl in my head.

Open the shutters. Let variation
abandon the swallows one by one.
How many summer dusks were needed
to make that single skimming form!
The very firefly kindles to its type.
Here is each evening's lesson. First
the hour, the setting. Only then
the human being, his white shirtsleeve
chalked among treetrunks, round a waist,
or lifted in an entrance. Look for him.
Be him.

Envoi for S.

Whom you saw mannerless and dull of heart,
Easy to fool, impossible to hurt,
I wore that fiction like a fine white shirt
And asked no favor but to act the part.

159

REMORA

This life is deep and dense
Beyond all seeing, yet one sees, in spite
Of being littler, a degree or two
Further than those one is attracted to.

Pea-brained, myopic, often brutal,
When chosen they have no defense—
A sucking sore there on the belly's pewter—
And where two go could be one's finer sense.

Who now descends from a machine
Plumed with bubbles, death in his right hand?
Lunge, numbskull! One, two, three worlds boil.
Thanks for the lift. There are other fish in the sea.

Still on occasion as by oversight
One lets be taken clinging fast
In heavenly sunshine to the corpse a slight
Tormented self, live, dapper, black-and-white.

MORNINGS IN A NEW HOUSE

And still at dawn the fire is lit
By whom a cold man hardly cares,
Reflection gliding up the legs of chairs,
Flue choking with the shock of it.

Next a frozen window thaws
In gradual slow stains of field,
Snow fence and birches more or less revealed.
This done, the brightness sheathes its claws.

The worst is over. Now between
His person and that tamed uprush
(Which to recall alone can make him flush)
Habit arranges the fire screen.*

Crewel-work. His mother as a child
Stitched giant birds and flowery trees
To dwarf a house, *her* mother's—see the chimney's
Puff of dull yarn! Still vaguely chilled,

Guessing how even then her eight
Years had foreknown him, nursed him, all,
Sewn his first dress, sung to him, let him fall,
Howled when his face chipped like a plate,

He stands there wondering until red
Infraradiance, wave on wave,
So enters each plume-petal's crazy weave,
Each worsted brick of the homestead,

*Days later. All framework & embroidery rather than any slower looking into things. Fire screen—screen *of* fire. The Valkyrie's baffle, pulsing at trance pitch, godgiven, elemental. Flames masking that cast-iron plaque—'contrecoeur' in French—which backs the hearth with charred Loves & Graces. Some such meaning might have caught, only I didn't wait, I settled for the obvious—by lamplight as it were. Oh well. Our white heats lead us on no less than words do. Both have been devices in their day.

That once more, deep indoors, blood's drawn,
The tiny needlewoman cries,
And to some faintest creaking shut of eyes
His pleasure and the doll's are one.

MATINEES

for David Kalstone

A gray maidservant lets me in
To Mrs Livingston's box. It's already begun!
The box is full of grownups. She sits me down
Beside her. Meanwhile a ravishing din

Swells from below—Scene One
Of *Das Rheingold*. The entire proscenium
Is covered with a rippling azure scrim.
The three sopranos dart hither and yon

On invisible strings. Cold lights
Cling to bare arms, fair tresses. Flat
And natural aglitter like paillettes
Upon the great green sonorous depths float

Until with pulsing wealth the house is filled,
No one believing, everybody thrilled.

Lives of the Great Composers make it sound
Too much like cooking: "Sore beset,
He put his heart's blood into that quintet . . ."
So let us try the figure turned around

As in some Lives of Obscure Listeners:
"The strains of Cimarosa and Mozart
Flowed through his veins, and fed his solitary heart.
Long beyond adolescence [One infers

Your elimination, sweet Champagne
Drunk between acts!] the aria's remote
Control surviving his worst interval,

Tissue of sound and tissue of the brain
Would coalesce, and what the Masters wrote
Itself compose his features sharp and small."

Hilariously Dr Scherer took the guise
Of a bland smoothshaven Alberich whose ageold
Plan had been to fill my tooth with gold.
Another whiff of laughing gas,

And the understanding was implicit
That we must guard each other, this gold and I,
Against amalgamation by
The elemental pit.

Vague as to what dentist and tooth "stood for,"
One patient dreamer gathered something more.
A voice said in the speech of birds,

"My father having tampered with your mouth,
From now on, metal, music, myth
Will seem to taint its words."

We love the good, said Plato? He was wrong.
We love as well the wicked and the weak.
Flesh hugs its shaved plush. Twenty-four-hour-long
Galas fill the hulk of the Comique.

Flesh knows by now what dishes to avoid,
Tries not to brood on bomb or heart attack.
Anatomy is destiny, said Freud.
Soul is the brilliant hypochondriac.

Soul will cough blood and sing, and softer sing,
Drink poison, breathe her joyous last, a waltz
Rubato from his arms who sobs and stays

Behind, death after death, who fairly melts
Watching her turn from him, restored, to fling
Kisses into the furnace roaring praise.

The fallen cake, the risen price of meat,
Staircase run ten times up and down like scales
(Greek proverb: He who has no brain has feet)—
One's household opera never palls or fails.

The pipes' aubade. Recitatives.—Come back!
—I'm out of pills!—We'd love to!—What?—*Nothing*,
Let me be!—No, no, I'll drink it black . . .
The neighbors' chorus. The quick darkening

In which a prostrate figure must inquire
With every earmark of its being meant
Why God in Heaven harries him/her so.

The love scene (often cut). The potion. The tableau:
Sleepers folded in a magic fire,
Tongues flickering up from humdrum incident.

When Jan Kiepura sang His Handsomeness
Of Mantua those high airs light as lust
Attuned one's bare throat to the dagger-thrust.
Living for them would have been death no less.

Or Lehmann's Marschallin!—heartbreak so shrewd,
So ostrich-plumed, one ached to disengage
Oneself from a last love, at center stage,
To the beloved's dazzled gratitude.

What havoc certain Saturday afternoons
Wrought upon a bright young person's morals
I now leave to the public to condemn.

The point thereafter was to arrange for one's
Own chills and fever, passions and betrayals,
Chiefly in order to make song of them.

Matinees

You and I, caro, seldom
Risk the real thing any more.
It's all too silly or too solemn.
Enough to know the score

From records or transcription
For our four hands. Old beauties, some
In advanced stages of decomposition,

Float up through the sustaining
Pedal's black and fluid medium.
Days like today

Even recur (wind whistling themes
From *Lulu,* and sun shining
On the rough Sound) when it seems
Kinder to remember than to play.

Dear Mrs Livingston,
I want to say that I am still in a daze
From yesterday afternoon.
I will treasure the experience always—

My very first Grand Opera! It was very
Thoughtful of you to invite
Me and am so sorry
That I was late, and for my coughing fit.

I play my record of the Overture
Over and over. I pretend
I am still sitting in the theatre.

I also wrote a poem which my Mother
Says I should copy out and send.
Ever gratefully, Your little friend . . .

THE SUMMER PEOPLE

> " . . . et l'hiver resterait la saison
> intellectuelle créatrice." MALLARMÉ

On our New England coast was once
A village white and neat
With Greek Revival houses,
Sailboats, a fishing fleet,

Two churches and two liquor stores,
An Inn, a Gourmet Shoppe,
A library, a pharmacy.
Trains passed but did not stop.

Gold Street was rich in neon,
Main Street in rustling trees
Untouched as yet by hurricanes
And the Dutch elm disease.

On Main the summer people
Took deep-rooted ease—
A leaf turned red, to town they'd head.
On Gold lived the Portuguese

Whose forebears had manned whalers.
Two years from the Azores
Saw you with ten gold dollars
Upon these fabled shores.

Feet still pace the whaler's deck
At the Caustic (Me.) Museum.
A small stuffed whale hangs overhead
As in the head a dream.

Slowly the fleet was shrinking.
The good-sized fish were few.
Town meetings closed and opened
With the question what to do.

The Summer People

Each year when manufacturers
Of chemicals and glues
Bid to pollute the harbor
It took longer to refuse.

Said Manuel the grocer,
"Vote for that factory,
And the summer people's houses
Will be up for sale, you'll see.

Our wives take in their laundry.
Our kids, they cut the grass
And baby-sit. The benefit
Comes home to all of us."

Someone else said, "Next winter
You'll miss that Chemical Plant."
Andrew breathed in Nora's ear:
"Go, grasshopper! Go, ant!"

These two were summer neighbors.
They loved without desire.
Both, now pushing fifty,
Had elsewhere played with fire.

Of all the summer people
Who dwelt in pigeonholes,
Old Navy or Young Married,
The Bad Sports, the Good Souls,

These were the Amusing,
The Unconventional ones—
Plus Andrew's Jane (she used a cane
And shook it at his puns)

And Nora's mother Margaret
With her dawn-colored hair,
Her novels laid in Europe
That she wrote in a garden chair.

"Where's Andrew?" Margaret queried
As Nora entered the room.
"Didn't he want to come over?
It seems to be my doom

To spend long lonely evenings.
Don't we *know* anyone?"
"Dozens of people, Mother."
"But none of them are fun!

The summer already seems endless
And it's only the first of July.
My eyes are too weak for reading
And I am too strong to cry.

I wish I weren't a widow,
I wish you weren't divorced—
Oh, by the way, I heard today
About a man named Frost

Who's bought the Baptist church
And means to do it over."
"Mother, he sounds like just the type
I don't need for a lover."

Andrew at the piano
Let the ice in his nightcap melt.
Mendelssohn's augmentations
Were very deeply felt.

Jane cleaned her paintbrushes
With fingers rheumatic and slow.
Their son came back from the movies,
She called a vague hello

But he'd bounded upstairs already,
Jarring three petals loose
From today's bunch of roses
Not dry yet—pink, cream, puce.

The Summer People

A young man spoke to Margaret
At a party: "Don't be bored.
I've read your books, I like your looks"—
Then vanished in the horde.

Her hostess said when questioned,
"Why, that's Interesting Jack Frost.
He's fixing up that eyesore
With no regard for cost.

Don't ask me where he comes from
Or why he settled here.
He's certainly attractive,
To judge by the veneer."

One thing led to another,
And long before summer's end,
Margaret, Nora, Andrew, Jane
Had found them a new friend.

Jack Frost was years older
Than his twenty-year-old face.
He loved four-hand piano
And gladly took the bass,

Loved also bridge but did not play
So well as to offend,
Loved to gossip, loved croquet,
His money loved to spend

On food and drink and flowers,
Loved entertaining most.
The happy few who'd been there knew
Him as a famous host.

The church was now a folly
Cloud-white and palest blue—
Lanterns, stained glass, mirrors,
Polar bear rugs, bamboo,

Armchairs of gleaming buffalo horn,
The titter of wind chimes,
A white cat, a blue cushion
Stitched with the cat's name, Grimes.

"Proud Grimes, proud loyal kitty,"
Jack said, "I love you best."
Two golden eyes were trimmed to slits,
Gorgeously unimpressed.

Ken the Japanese "houseboy"
(Though silver-haired and frail)
Served many a curious hot hors d'oeuvre
And icy cold cocktail.

The new friends, that first evening,
Sat on till half past two.
"This man," said Andrew on the street,
"Is too good to be true.

One views with faint misgivings
The bounty of the young."
"Speak for yourself," said Nora
Or the Cointreau on her tongue.

"Well, *I* think he's enchanting,"
Said Margaret, "and what's more
In the long run he'll find, for fun,
No one to match us four."

October came too quickly,
The leaves turned red and sere,
Time for the summer people
To pack up and call it a year.

In the mind's mouth summers later
Ken's farewell banquet melts.
Where would Jack spend the winter?
Why, here of course—where else?

The Summer People

"Stay here all winter? Really,
The things some people do!"
"Whither thou goest, Margaret,
To thee I will be true."

"Come see us in the city."
"My lovely Nora, no.
Too full of dull, dull people
And dirty, dirty snow."

"Come see *us* in Barbados."
"Forgive me, dearest Jane.
I've planned a Northern winter."
So they cajoled in vain.

The next days Jack lay drowsing,
Grimes in the bend of his knees.
He woke one dusk to eat a rusk
And smile at the bare trees.

The first huge flakes descended
Hexagonal, unique.
The panes put forth white leafage.
The harbor froze in a week.

The shrieking children skated
Upon its harsh white jewel,
Whose parents stayed indoors and paid
Outrageous bills for fuel.

Great lengths of gnarled crystal
Glittered from porch and eave.
It was, in short, a winter
You had to see to believe.

Whole nights, a tower window
Threw light upon the storm.
"Jack's sure artistic," Manuel said,
"But how does he keep warm?"

Ken climbed the stair one March dusk.
"Dear Jack-san, now am ord,
Dream of my Kyushu virrage
Where nobody catch cord."

"Together, Ken, we'll go there,
But for the moment stay.
What would I do without you?"
Ken bowed and turned away.

Jack stood up. The cat scuttled
Discreetly out of sight.
Jack's eyes were wet. Pride and regret
Burned in his heart all night.

A mild sun rose next morning.
The roofs began to steam
Where snow had melted. Winter
Was ending like a dream.

Alerted and elated
The summer friends came back.
Their exile had been tiresome,
Each now confessed to Jack.

His garden made them welcome;
Ken had spent May on his knees
Among the plots. From Chinese pots
On the church porch small trees

Rose thick with purple blossoms
Pendulous as Turks.
Said Andrew gravely, "I have seen
The fuchsia, and it works."

That summer was the model
For several in a row—
High-water marks of humor
And humankindness, no

The Summer People

Discord at cards, at picnics,
Charades or musicales.
Their faces bright with pleasure might
Not have displeased Frans Hals.

Jane, speaking of pictures,
Had started one of Grimes
Drugged on Jack's lap. Those sessions
Made for the merriest times.

Margaret brought out her gripping
Stories of love and war,
Peking and Nice. They held their peace
Who'd heard them told before.

Nora, one August afternoon,
Burst in with currant fool
Enough for the whole village.
Its last sweet molecule

Eaten, they blushed like truants.
"Shame on us every one,"
Jane sighed, "we've got no fiber."
And Margaret: "Oh, the fun!

Let's stay for Christmas. Andrew,
You can play Santa Claus!"
Jack gave a cry. Into his thigh
The cat had dug its claws.

Jane's canvas, scarred and peeling
Turned up at the village fair
The other day. I'm sad to say
It found a customer.

The Chemical Plant director
Bought it for his wife
To overpaint with symbols
Blunt as her palette knife.

They're a perfectly nice couple
So long as you steer clear
Of art and politics and such—
But to resume. That year

Jack's friends did stay for Christmas,
The next year into Lent,
A third year stayed all winter
To their own astonishment.

Logs burned, the sparks flew upward.
The whiteness when they woke
Struck them as of a genius
Positively baroque,

Invention's breast and plumage,
Flights of the midnight Swan . . .
The facts are in Margaret's journal
To be published when she's gone.

I should perhaps have trusted
To dry-eyed prose like hers.
The meter grows misleading,
Given my characters.

For figures in a ballad
Lend themselves to acts
Passionate and simple.
A bride weeps. A tree cracks.

A young king, an old outlaw
Whose temperament inclines
To strife where breakers thunder
Bleeds between the lines.

But I have no such hero,
No fearful deeds—unless
We count their quiet performance
By Time or Tenderness.

The Summer People

These two are the past masters
Of rime, tone, overtone.
They write upon our faces
Until the pen strikes bone.

Time passes softly, scarcely
Felt by me or you.
And then, at an odd moment,
Tenderness passes, too.

That January midday
Jack's head fell to his knee.
Margaret stopped in mid-sentence—
Whatever could it be?

"He's sound asleep," said Nora.
"So clever of him. If
Only I were! Your stories
Bore everybody stiff."

"What can she mean," said Margaret,
"Speaking to me like that?"
"I mean you're gaga, Mother."
"And you, my child, are fat."

Jack murmured in his slumber,
"I didn't sleep a wink
All during last night's blizzard.
Where am I? Where's my drink?"

His eyes flew wide. "I'm sorry,
I'm sick, I have to go."
He took his coat and tottered
Out into windless snow.

The dogwood at the corner,
Unbending in a burst
Of diamond levity, let drop:
Old friend, think! First things first,

176

Not June in January—
"Be still!" cried Jack, and bit
His stupid tongue. A snowflake stung
Silence back into it.

Ken helped him up the tower stair,
"Rie down, Jack-san, now rest."
He fell among white blankets,
Grimes heavy on his chest.

Margaret went round next morning
And rang. No one replied.
She found Ken sleeping on the stair,
A wineglass at his side.

A white blur sped to meet her—
Was it that ghastly cat?
Grimes spat, crouched, sprang and sank a fang
Into her, just like that!

She screamed. A stern young doctor,
Summoned out of the void,
Dressed her wound, then telephoned
To have the cat destroyed.

Jack flew to the Police Chief,
Called the SPCA,
Despairing thought that Margaret
Herself might save the day.

She kept him standing, coldly
Displayed her bandaged calf.
He spoiled it all by failing
To check a thoughtless laugh.

Two men with gloves were waiting.
They caught Grimes in a sack.
Two good whiffs of ether
And his gold eyes shut on Jack.

That same night, Grimes in ermine
And coronet of ice
Called him by name, cried vengeance,
Twitching his long tail twice.

Jack woke in pitch dark, burning,
Freezing, leapt dry-lipped
From bed, threw clothes on, neither
Packed nor reflected, slipped

Money between pages
Of Ken's dog-eared almanac,
Then on the sleeping village
Forever turned his back.

He must have let a month go by
Before he sent them all
Postcards of some Higher Thing—
The Jungfrau, white and tall.

"Well, that answers our question,"
Said Margaret looking grim.
They dealt with Jack from then on
By never mentioning him.

Languid as convalescents,
Dreading the color green,
They braced themselves for summer's
Inexorable routine.

Andrew at the piano,
Six highballs gone or more,
Played Brahms, his "venerable beads"
Fixed on the flickering score.

Kneeling in her muggy
Boxwood garden Jane
Stopped weeding, tried to rise
But could not move for pain.

She saw her son's tanned fingers
Lowering the blind
Of an attic window.
She did not know his mind.

Croquet and hectic banter
From Margaret's back yard
Broke upon her twinges.
"*En,*" shrieked Nora, "*garde!*"

"Oh God, this life's so pointless,
So wearing," Margaret said.
"You're telling me," Andrew agreed.
"High time we both were dead."

"It *is*. I have pills—let's take them!"
He looked at her with wit.
"Just try. You know we'd never
Hear the end of it."

Their laughter floated on the dusk.
Ken thought of dropping in,
But his nails were cracked and dirty
And his breath smelled of gin.

"Missed you at Town Meeting
Last night," said Manuel
As Nora fingered honeydews.
"Things didn't go too well.

Fact is, the Plant got voted in.
I call it a downright
Pity you summer people
Didn't care enough to fight."

"Manuel, there have been winters
We stayed here," Nora said.
"That makes us year-round people."
The grocer scratched his head.

"I guess I don't mean season
So much as a point of view."
It made her mad. She'd meant to add,
"And we do care, we *do*,"

But it was too late, she didn't,
Didn't care one bit.
Manuel counted out her change:
". . . *and* ten. Will that be it?"

"Insufferable rudeness!
Of course by now it's clear,"
Said Margaret, laying down her trumps,
"We must all get out of here."

"We go next week," admitted
Jane with a guilty air.
"Old friends in Locust Valley
Keep asking us down there."

"Besides," said Andrew quickly,
"This climate's bothersome.
I may take Jane to Port-of-Spain—
All *my* roads lead to rum."

"So they do. Well, that's lovely,
Leaving us in the lurch,"
Said Nora, "just like what's-his-name
Who had the Baptist church."

"The summer's over," said Margaret.
"But you misunderstood:
I meant this town was ruined.
We must all get out for good."

Ken wrapped some Canton saucers
Like a conspirator,
To be exchanged for credit
At the corner liquor store.

September. Dismal rainstorms
Made everything a blur,
Lashed Margaret into action—
City life for her!

"I'll stay up here," said Nora,
"A month or two. I need
Time to think things over,
Listen to records, read."

She drove home from Caustic
Where Margaret caught her plane.
The windshield streamed in silence,
The wipers thrashed in vain.

October. Early twilights.
To the wharf came a blue
And silver haul of fish too small
For anything but glue.

The boatyard was a boneyard,
Bleached hull, moon-eaten chain.
The empty depot trembled
At the scream of a passing train.

Nora long past midnight
Lay rereading *Emma*,
Unmoved for once by a daughter's
Soon-to-be-solved dilemma.

And late dawns. The first victim
Of Main Street's seventeen
Doomed elms awoke and feebly shook
Its sparrow-tambourine.

In the November mildness
Rose delicate green spears—
Spring flowers Ken had planted.
His small eyes filled with tears:

The Summer People

They were coming up too early!
He sniffed and went indoors.
He dusted all the objects,
Polished the bare floors,

Bathed and oiled his person;
Now put on his best clothes,
Thought up a huge sweet cocktail,
And sipping at it chose

The first words of a letter
He had long meant to write.
But wait, his glass was empty—
A foolish oversight.

Nora heard him coughing.
She stopped her evening stroll
And went to see. With courtesy
Both sinister and droll

Ken bowed low, made her welcome,
Concocted a new drink.
Darkly hilarious he said,
"Rong rife!" and gave a wink.

One didn't need to be Nora
To see that things weren't right.
In his brown silk kimono
Ken sat there high as a kite.

His talk was incoherent:
Jack—his mother's loom—
The weather—his green island—
Flowers he'd not see bloom—

The dead cat—a masked actor—
Ghosts up in the hills . . .
And then those frightful spasms
Followed by small white pills.

Nora thought food might help him
And ran back for a cup
Of homemade soup. He took a sip,
Set down the cup, got up:

"Dear Missy-san, too sorty.
Night-night now. Kissing hand."
This done, Ken headed for the stair,
Though hardly able to stand.

Next day she found him lying
Cold on his bed. "I knew,
I *knew!*" sobbed Nora over the phone.
"But what was there to do?

He wasn't kin or even friend,
Just old and sick, poor dear.
It was his right to take his life,
Not mine to interfere."

"Exactly," said her mother.
"I'll come tomorrow. Jack?
Try the address on Ken's letter.
A wire may bring him back."

It did not. The two ladies
Arranged the funeral,
Then sat at home in silence
Deeper than I can tell.

Jack sent a check weeks later
And wrote them from Tibet
A long sad charming letter,
But friendship's sun had set.

December. "I think sometimes,"
Said Margaret dreamily,
"That Jack was a delusion
Of the whole community.

No reasonable adult
Starts acting like a child.
How else can you explain it?
He had us all beguiled."

Nora looked up. The mirror
Struck her a glancing blow.
Her hair once blonde as summer
Was dull and streaked with snow.

"Oh tell me, Mother, tell me
Where do the years go?
I'm old, my life is ending!"
"Baby, I know, I know."

As soon as they were calmer,
"I also," Margaret said,
"Know what to do about it.
So get up from that bed.

I know a clever fairy
Who puts gold back in hair.
I know of jets to Rio.
It will be summer there."

Come May, Ken's garden blossomed
In memory of him—
Hyacinth, narcissus
White as seraphim.

Jane and Andrew saw it.
They'd driven up to sell
Their house at a tidy profit
To the Head of Personnel.

It had grown so big, so empty.
Their lawn was choked with weeds,
Their son in California
Barefoot, all beard and beads.

They stood among Ken's flowers
Gazing without a word.
Jane put her hand in Andrew's.
The cat in heaven purred.

And then a faint piano
Sounded—from where? They tried
The door, it floated open,
Inviting them inside.

Sitting at the keyboard
In a cloud of brilliant motes
A boy they'd both seen somewhere
Was playing random notes.

He rose as if uncertain
Whether to speak or run.
Jane said, "I know who you are,
You're Joey, Manuel's son,

Who used to cut the grass for us.
Look at you, grown so tall!"
He grinned. "I won a scholarship
At M.I.T. this fall

To study cybernetics
And flute—it's worth a try.
I used to come and talk to Ken.
I miss that little guy."

"One by one, like swallows . . ."
Said Andrew in the gloom
That fell when Joe departed.
"Dear God, look at this room."

Full ashtrays, soft-drink bottles
Told an artless tale
Of adolescent revels.
Tan stacks of ninth-class mail

Lay tumbled helter-skelter.
A chill in the stirred air
Sent Jane outdoors and Andrew
To brave the tower stair.

Moon after moon had faded
The papers on Jack's desk:
Unfinished calculation,
Doodle and arabesque.

One window framed the sunset
Transfiguring Main Street,
Its houses faintly crimson
But upright in defeat.

The other faced the harbor.
Lights of the Chemical Plant
Gloated over water.
"The grasshopper, the ant,"

Breathed Andrew, recollecting
His long ago remark,
Then shut both views behind him
And felt his way down in dark.

From Braving the Elements (1972)

LOG

Then when the flame forked like a sudden path
I gasped and stumbled, and was less.
Density pulsing upward, gauze of ash,
Dear light along the way to nothingness,
What could be made of you but light, and this?

AFTER THE FIRE

Everything changes; nothing does. I am back,
The doorbell rings, my heart leaps out of habit,
But it is only Kleo—how thin, how old!—
Trying to smile, lips chill as the fallen dusk.

She has brought a cake "for tomorrow"
As if tomorrows were still memorable.
We sit down in the freshly-painted hall
Once used for little dinners. (The smoke cleared
On no real damage, yet I'd wanted changes,
Balcony glassed in, electric range,
And wrote to have them made after the fire.)
Now Kleo's eyes begin to stream in earnest—
Tears of joy? Ah, troubles too, I fear.
Her old mother has gone off the deep end.

From their basement window the yiayia, nearly ninety,
Hurls invective at the passing scene,
Tea bags as well, the water bill, an egg
For emphasis. A strange car stops outside?
She cackles *Here's the client! Paint your face,*
Putana! to her daughter moistening
With tears the shirt she irons. Or locks her out
On her return from watering, with tears,
My terrace garden. (I will see tomorrow
The white oleander burst from its pot in the rains.)
Nor is darling Panayióti, Kleo's son,
Immune. Our entire neighbourhood now knows
As if they hadn't years before
That he is a *Degenerate!* a *Thieving*
Faggot! just as Kleo is a *Whore!*

I press Kleo's cold hand and wonder
What could the poor yiayia have done
To deserve this terrible gift of hindsight,

These visions that possess her of a past
When Kleo really was a buxom armful
And "Noti" cruised the Naval Hospital,
Slim then, with teased hair. Now he must be forty,
Age at which degeneration takes
Too much of one's time and strength and money.
My eyes brim with past evenings in this hall,
Gravy-spattered cloth, candles minutely
Guttering in the love-blinded gaze.
The walls' original oldfashioned colors,
Cendre de rose, warm flaking ivory—
Colors last seen as by that lover's ghost
Stumbling downstairs wound in a sheet of flame—
Are hidden now forever but not lost
Beneath this quiet sensible light gray.

Kleo goes on. The yiayia's *warm,*
What can it mean? She who sat blanketed
In mid-July now burns all day,
Eats only sugar, having ascertained
Poison in whatever Kleo cooks.
Kill me, there'll be an autopsy,
Putana, matricide, I've seen to that!
I mention my own mother's mother's illness,
Querulous temper, lucid shame.
Kleo says weeping that it's not the same,
There's nothing wrong, according to the doctor,
Just that she's old and merciless. And warm.

Next day I visit them. Red-eyed Kleo
Lets me in. Beyond her, bedclothes disarrayed,
The little leaden oven-rosy witch
Fastens her unrecognizing glare
Onto the lightest line that I can spin.
"It's me, yiayia! Together let us plumb
Depths long dry"—getting no further, though,
Than Panayióti's anaconda arms:

"Ah Monsieur Tzim, bon zour et bon retour!
Excuse mon déshabillé. Toute la nuit
Z'ai décoré l'église pour la fête
Et fait l'amour, le prêtre et moi,
Dans une alcove derrière la Sainte Imaze.
Tiens, z'ai un cadeau pour toi,
Zoli foulard qui me va pas du tout.
Mais prends-le donc, c'est pas volé—
Ze ne suis plus voleur, seulement volaze!"

Huge, powerful, bland, he rolls his eyes and r's.
Glints of copper wreathe his porcelain brow
Like the old-time fuses here, that blow so readily.
I seem to know that crimson robe,
And on his big fat feet—my slippers, ruined.
Still, not to complicate affairs,
Remembering also the gift of thumb-sized garnet
Bruises he clasped round Aleko's throat,
I beam with gratitude. Meanwhile
Other translated objects one by one
Peep from hiding: teapot, towel, transistor.
Upon the sideboard an old me
Scissored from its glossy tavern scene—
I know that bare arm too, flung round my shoulder—
Buckles against a ruby glass ashtray.
(It strikes me now, as happily it did not
The insurance company, that P caused the fire.
Kleo's key borrowed for a rendezvous,
A cigarette left burning . . . Never mind.)
Life like the bandit Somethingopoulos
Gives to others what it takes from us.

Some of those embers can't be handled yet.

I mean to ask whose feast it is today
But the room brightens, the yiayia shrieks my name—
It's Tzimi! He's returned!
—And with that she returns to human form,

The snuffed-out candle-ends grow tall and shine,
Dead flames encircle us, which cannot harm,
The table's spread, she croons, and I
Am kneeling pressed to her old burning frame.

DAYS OF 1935

Ladder horned against moonlight,
Window hoisted stealthily—
That's what I'd steel myself at night
To see, or sleep to see.

My parents were out partying,
My nurse was old and deaf and slow.
Way off in the servants' wing
Cackled a radio.

On the Lindbergh baby's small
Cold features lay a spell, a swoon.
It seemed entirely plausible
For my turn to come soon,

For a masked and crouching form
Lithe as tiger, light as moth,
To glide towards me, clap a firm
Hand across my mouth,

Then sheer imagination ride
Off with us in its old jalopy,
Trailing bedclothes like a bride
Timorous but happy.

A hundred tenuous dirt roads
Dew spangles, lead to the web's heart.
That whole pale night my captor reads
His brow's unwrinkling chart.

Dawn. A hovel in the treeless
Trembling middle of nowhere,
Hidden from the world by palace
Walls of dust and glare.

A lady out of *Silver Screen,*
Her careful rosebud chewing gum,
Seems to expect us, lets us in,
Nods her platinum

Spit curls deadpan (I will wait
Days to learn what makes her smile)
At a blue enamel plate
Of cold greens I can smell—

But swallow? Never. The man's face
Rivets me, a lightning bolt.
Lean, sallow, lantern-jawed, he lays
Pistol and cartridge belt

Between us on the oilskin (I
Will relive some things he did
Until I die, until I die)
And clears his throat: "Well, Kid,

You've figured out what's happening.
We don't mean to hurt you none
Unless we have to. Everything
Depends on, number one,

How much you're worth to your old man,
And, number two, no more of this—"
Meaning my toothprints on his hand,
Indenture of a kiss.

With which he fell upon the bed
And splendidly began to snore.
"Please, I'm sleepy too," I said.
She pointed to the floor.

The rag rug, a rainbow threadbare,
Was soft as down. For good or bad
I felt her watching from her chair
As no one ever had.

Their names were Floyd and Jean. I guess
They lived in what my parents meant
By sin: unceremoniousness
Or common discontent.

"Gimme—Wait—Hey, watch that gun—
Why don't these dumb matches work—
See you later—Yeah, have fun—
Wise guy—Floozie—Jerk—"

Or else he bragged of bygone glories,
Stores robbed, cars stolen, dolls betrayed,
Escape from two reformatories.
Said Jean, "Wish you'd of stayed."

To me they hardly spoke, just watched
Or gave directions in dumb show.
I nodded back like one bewitched
By a violent glow.

Each morning Floyd went for a ride
To post another penciled note.
Indignation nationwide
Greeted what he wrote.

Each afternoon, brought papers back.
One tabloid's whole front page was spanned
By the headline bold and black:
FIEND ASKS 200 GRAND.

Photographs too. My mother gloved,
Hatted, bepearled, chin deep in fur.
Dad glowering—was it true he loved
Others beside her?

Eerie, speaking likenesses.
One positively heard her mild
Voice temper some slow burn of his,
"Not before the child."

The child. That population map's
Blanknesses and dots were me!
Mine, those swarming eyes and lips,
Centers of industry

Italics under which would say
(And still do now and then, I fear)
Is This Child Alive Today?
Last Hopes Disappear.

Toy ukelele, terrorstruck
Chord, the strings so taut, so few—
Tingling I hugged my pillow. *Pluck*
Some deep nerve went. I knew

That life was fiction in disguise.
My teeth said, chattering in Morse,
"Are you a healthy wealthy wise
Red-blooded boy? Of course?

Then face the music. Stay. Outwit
Everyone. Captivity
Is beckoning—make a dash for it!
It will set you free."

Sometimes as if I were not there
He put his lips against her neck.
Her head lolled sideways, just like Claire
Coe in "Tehuantepec."

Then both would send me looks so heaped
With a lazy, scornful mirth,
This was growing up, I hoped,
The first flushed fruits of earth.

One night I woke to hear the room
Filled with crickets—no, bedsprings.
My eyes dilated in the gloom,
My ears made out things.

Jean: The kid, he's still awake . . .
Floyd: Time he learned . . . Oh baby . . . God . . .
Their prone tango, for my sake,
Grew intense and proud.

And one night—pure "Belshazzar's Feast"
When the slave-girl is found out—
She cowered, face a white blaze ("Beast!")
From his royal clout.

Mornings, though, she came and went,
Buffed her nails and plucked her brows.
What had those dark doings meant?
Less than the fresh bruise

Powdered over on her cheek.
I couldn't take my eyes away.
Let hers meet them! Let her speak!
She put down *Photoplay:*

"Do you know any stories, Kid?
Real stories—but not real, I mean.
Not just dumb things people did.
Wouldja tell one to Jean?"

I stared at her—*she* was the child!—
And a tale came back to me.
Bluebeard. At its end she smiled
Half incredulously.

I spun them out all afternoon.
Wunspontime, I said and said . . .
The smile became a dainty yawn
Rose-white and rose-red.

The little mermaid danced on knives,
The beauty slept in her thorn bower.
Who knows but that our very lives
Depend on such an hour?

The fisherman's hut became Versailles
Because he let the dolphin go . . .
Jean's lids have shut. I'm lonely. I
Am pausing on tiptoe

To marvel at the shimmer breath
Inspires along your radii,
Spider lightly running forth
To kiss the simple fly

Asleep. A chance to slip the net,
Wriggle down the dry stream bed,
Now or never! This child cannot.
An iridescent thread

Binds him to her slumber deep
Within a golden haze made plain
Precisely where his fingertip
Writes on the dusty pane

In spit his name, address, age nine
—Which the newspapers and such
Will shortly point to as a fine
Realistic touch.

Grown up, he thinks how S, T, you—
Second childhood's alphabet
Still unmastered, it is true,
Though letters come—have yet

Touched his heart, occasioned words
Not quickened by design alone,
Responses weekly winging towards
Your distance from his own,

Distance that much more complex
For its haunting ritornel:
Things happen to a child who speaks
To strangers, mark it well!

Thinks how you or V—where does
It end, will *any*one have done?—
Taking the wheel (cf. those "Days
Of 1971")

Have driven, till his mother's Grade
A controls took charge, or handsome
Provisions which his father made
Served once again as ransom,

Driven your captive far enough
For the swift needle on the gauge
To stitch with delicate kid stuff
His shoddy middle age.

Here was Floyd. The evening sun
Filled his eyes with funny light.
"Junior, you'll be home real soon."
To Jean, "Tomorrow night."

What was happening? Had my parents
Paid? pulled strings? Or maybe I
Had failed in manners, or appearance?
Must this be goodbye?

I'd hoped I was worth more than crime
Itself, which never paid, could pay.
Worth more than my own father's time
Or mother's negligée

Undone where dim ends barely met,
This being a Depression year . . .
I'd hoped, I guess, that they would let
Floyd and Jean keep me here.

We ate in silence. He would stop
Munching and gaze into the lamp.
She wandered out on the dark stoop.
The night turned chill and damp.

When she came in, she'd caught a bug.
She tossed alone in the iron bed.
Floyd dropped beside me on the rug;
Growled, "Sleep." I disobeyed.

Commenced a wary, mortal heat
Run neck by nose. Small fingers felt,
Sore point of all that wiry meat,
A nipple's tender fault.

Time stopped. His arm somnambulist
Had circled me, warm, salt as blood.
Mine was the future in his fist
To get at if I could,

While his heart beat like a drum
And *Oh baby* faint and hoarse
Echoed from within his dream . . .
The next day Jean was worse

—Or I was. Dawn discovered me
Sweating on my bedroom floor.
Was there no curbing fantasy
When one had a flair?

Came those nights to end the tale.
I shrank to see the money tumble,
All in 20s, from a teal
Blue Studebaker's rumble

Down a slope of starlit brush.
Sensed with anguish the foreseen
Net of G-men, heard the hush
Deepen, then Floyd's voice ("Jean,

Baby, we've been doublecrossed!")
Drowned out by punctual crossfire
That left the pillow hot and creased.
By three o'clock, by four,

Days of 1935

They stood in handcuffs where the hunt
Was over among blood-smeared rocks
—Whom I should not again confront
Till from the witness-box

I met their stupid, speechless gaze.
How empty they appeared, how weak
By contrast with my opening phrase
As I began to speak:

"You I adored I now accuse . . ."
Would imagination dare
Follow that sentence like a fuse
Sizzling towards the Chair?

See their bodies raw and swollen
Sagging in a skein of smoke?
The floor was reeling where I'd fallen.
Even my old nurse woke

And took me in her arms. I pressed
My guilty face against the void
Warmed and scented by her breast.
Jean, I whispered, Floyd.

A rainy day. The child is bored.
While Emma bakes he sits, half-grown.
The kitchen dado is of board
Painted like board. Its grain

Shiny buff on cinnamon
Mimics the real, the finer grain.
He watches icing sugar spin
Its thread. He licks in vain

Heavenly flavors from a spoon.
Left in the metallic bowl
Is a twenty-five watt moon.
Somewhere rings a bell.

202

Wet walks from the East porch lead
Down levels manicured and rolled
To a small grove where pets are laid
In shallow emerald.

The den lights up. A Sazerac
Helps his father face the *Wall
Street Journal*. Jules the colored (black)
Butler guards the hall.

Tel & Tel executives,
Heads of Cellophane or Tin,
With their animated wives
Are due on the 6:10.

Upstairs in miles of spangled blue
His mother puts her make-up on.
She kisses him sweet dreams, but who—
Floyd and Jean are gone—

Who will he dream of? True to life
He's played them false. A golden haze
Past belief, past disbelief . . .
Well. Those were the days.

18 WEST 11TH STREET

a house in Manhattan,
our home until I was five, carelessly exploded by the
'Weathermen'—young, bomb-making activists—in 1970

In what at least
Seemed anger the Aquarians in the basement
Had been perfecting a device

For making sense to us
If only briefly and on pain
Of incommunication ever after.

Now look who's here. Our prodigal
Sunset. Just passing through from Isfahan.
Filled by him the glass

Disorients. The swallow-flights
Go word by numbskull word
—Rebellion . . . Pentagon . . . Black Studies—

Crashing into irreality,
Plumage and parasites
Plus who knows what of the reptilian,

Till wit turns on the artificial lights
Or heaven changes. The maid,
Silent, pale as any victim,

Comes in, identifies;
Yet brings new silver, gives rise to the joint,
The presidency's ritual eclipse.

Take. Eat. His body to our lips. The point
Was anger, brother? Love? Dear premises
Vainly exploded, vainly dwelt upon.

Item: the carpet
Identical bouquets on black, rose-dusted
Face in fifty funeral parlors,

Scentless and shaven, wall-to-wall
Extravagance without variety . . .
That morning's buzzing vacuum be fed

By ash of metropolitan evening's
Smoker inveterate between hot bouts
Of gloating over scrollwork,

The piano (three-legged by then like a thing in a riddle)
Fingered itself provocatively. Tones
Jangling whose tuner slept, moon's camphor mist

On the parterre compounding
Chromatic muddles which the limpid trot
Flew to construe. Up from camellias

Sent them by your great-great-grandfather,
Ghosts in dwarf sateen and miniver
Flitted once more askew

Through *Les Sylphides*. The fire was dead. Each summer,
While onto white keys miles from here
Warm salt chords kept breaking, snapping the strings,

The carpet—its days numbered—
Hatched another generation
Of strong-jawed, light-besotted saboteurs.

A mastermind
Kept track above the mantel. The cold caught,
One birthday in its shallows, racked

18 West 11 Street

The weak frame, glazed with sleet
Overstuffed aunt and walnut uncle. Book
You could not read. Some utterly

Longed-for present meeting other eyes'
Blue arsenal of homemade elegies,
Duds every one. The deed

Diffused. Your breakfast *Mirror* put
Late to bed, a fever
Flashing through the veins of linotype:

NIX ON PEACE BID   PROPHET STONED
FIVE FEARED DEAD IN BOMBED DWELLING
—Bulletin-pocked columns, molten font

Features would rise from, nose for news
Atwitch, atchoo, God bless you!
Brought to your senses (five feared? not one bit)

Who walking home took in
The ruin. The young linden opposite
Shocked leafless. Item: the March dawn.

Shards of a blackened witness still in place.
The charred ice-sculpture garden
Beams fell upon. The cold blue searching beams.

Then all you sought
No longer, B came bearing. An arrangement
In time known simply as That June—

Fat snifter filled with morbidest
Possibly meat-eating flowers,
So hairy-stemmed, red-muscled, not to be pressed.

Pinhead notions underwater, yours,
Quicksilvered them afresh.
You let pass certain telltale prints

Left upon her in the interim
By that winter's person, where he touched her.
Still in her life now, was he, feeling the dim

Projection of your movie on his sheet?
Feeling how you reached past B towards him,
Brothers in grievance? But who grieves!

The night she left ("One day you'll understand")
You stood under the fruitless tree. The streetlight
Cast false green fires about, a tragic

Carpet of shadows of blossoms, shadows of leaves.
You understood. You would not seek rebirth
As a Dalmatian stud or Tiny Tim.

Discolorations from within, dry film
Run backwards, parching, scorching, to consume
Whatever filled you to the brim,

Fierce tongue, black
Fumes massing forth once more on
Waterstilts that fail them. The

Commissioner unswears his oath. Sea serpent
Hoses recoil, the siren drowns in choking
Wind. The crowd has thinned to a

Coven rigorously chosen from so many
Called. Our instant trance. The girl's
Appearance now among us, as foreseen

18 West 11 Street

Naked, frail but fox-eyed, head to toe
(Having passed through the mirror)
Adorned with heavy shreds of ribbon

Sluggish to bleed. She stirs, she moans the name
Adam. And is *gone*. By her own
Broom swept clean, god, stop, behind this

Drunken backdrop of debris, airquake,
Flame in bloom—a pigeon's throat
Lifting, the puddle

Healed. To let:
Cream paint, brown ivy, brickflush. Eye
Of the old journalist unwavering

Through gauze. Forty-odd years gone by.
Toy blocks. Church bells. Original vacancy.
O deepening spring.

WILLOWWARE CUP

Mass hysteria, wave after breaking wave
Blueblooded Cantonese upon these shores

Left the gene pool Lux-opaque and smoking
With dimestore mutants. One turned up today.

Plum in bloom, pagoda, blue birds, plume of willow—
Almost the replica of a prewar pattern—

The same boat bearing the gnat-sized lovers away,
The old bridge now bent double where her father signals

Feebly, as from flypaper, minding less and less.
Two smaller retainers with lanterns light him home.

Is that a scroll he carries? He must by now be immensely
Wise, and have given up earthly attachments, and all that.

Soon, of these May mornings, rising in mist, he will ask
Only to blend—like ink in flesh, blue anchor

Needled upon drunkenness while its destroyer
Full steam departs, the stigma throbbing, intricate—

Only to blend into a crazing texture.
You are far away. The leaves tell what they tell.

But this lone, chipped vessel, if it fills,
Fills for you with something warm and clear.

Around its inner horizon the old odd designs
Crowd as before, and seem to concentrate on you.

They represent, I fancy, a version of heaven
In its day more trouble to mend than to replace:

Steep roofs aslant, minutely tiled;
Tilted honeycombs, thunderhead blue.

BANKS OF A STREAM WHERE CREATURES BATHE

Through slits in the plantain leaf,
Celestial surge!
The fabulous old Goat
Extends nightlong

Ancien régime
Propositions. Stick with him
And you'll be wearing diamonds . . .
Barely relenting

You of the cool breast
Unclasp the rivière.
Facets reassembled
Pulse and scatter.

The courts of heaven
In sparkling shambles
Struggle against you
Like a shack on poles.

I can't compete.
Giving of my very
Self, I've seen you
Clouded by the gift.

You want diversions
Deeply pure, is that it?
Trust me. I keep trying
Not to break down.

I know the hoof
Imprinted on my clay,
His bulk and poise
Who drinks you, enters you;

And hold you close,
Too close to make the best
Of that recurrently
Real beast in you.

At dawn asleep
In fairness take these colors.
Do not sweep me
Downstream with the stars.

IN NINE SLEEP VALLEY

I
Trying to read in Nature's book
The pages (canyon forest landslide lake)
Turn as the road does, the stock characters
Come and (marmot mallard moose)

Go too quickly to believe in. Look,
I'm told, but many of the words have wings
Or run to type in small fleet herds
No question of retaining—what's the use!

Coming meanwhile to believe in you,
Fluent and native. Only read aloud
Do the words stay with me, through
Whose roots those flat clear vowels flow

To mirror, surfacing, the things they mean:
Blue heron, mountain, antelope, spruce, cloud.

2
Yesterday's flower, American Beauty
Crimson and sweet all night in the city,
Limp now, changed in import as in color,
Floats behind us in the tinkling cooler.

Yesterday also Robert Kennedy's
Train of refrigerated dignitaries
Last seen on TV burying Dr King
Wormed its way to Arlington Cemetery.

The beauty I mean to press fading
Between these lines is yours, and the misleading
Sweetness, leaves and portals of a body
Ajar, cool, nodding at the wheel already.

212

3

Dawn, the muted chirr and squeal—dream axle
Grinding your jaws? I mind for you
Prematurely.
In our roof are swallows,
Young ones breast to breast.

4

Next a high pool deep blue very hot
Illumination of the brimstone text
Beyond your windburned lips panted and steamed
As did the spring left far below with death,

Its green rank to which we should return,
Two good men in high places out of breath
Less now than ant or tick the noon's cold bird
Lured to cast its ravenous milligram

Into the scale, and the small window steamed
Where I sat alone high blue
Taking stock of wing and wishbone stewed
At giddily low temperature—

Ice in the marrow of a star so pure
So beyond history, the eye-searing water
Onion or headline or your fine print drew
Dried in a wink, quick sleights of altitude.

5

Each day at dusk we roam the sage.
Heavenly repertory, bleakest rage

Bleeding to sour gleams, hard-edge jubilance,
All encompassed by one lariat glance.

The peaks turn baseless as the fear
That you will tell me what I live to hear.

Look, is all. The cabin. Look. The river.
Aspens glowing, site gloomed over.

Look. Out of thin air old gods (plume, hide, bead)
Appear to weigh your offerings of seed.

A leathery prospector god's pans fill
With foolsgold facets of my blackbird's trill.

Then all take umbrage in a blue
The silence positively ripples through.

6

From glade by river to a further day's
Thirst-crazed hilltop the abandoned cabin
Kept wandering like a mind with its few same
Obsessions, robin's nest and dish of rust,
Cracked pane dingily festooned,
Roof leaking sky, the same forty year old
Illustrated fictions sticking to its ribs

Where once again, the flask uncorked, two rooms
Are won back to this world,
Book by loaf a whole life dreams itself
From the foundation, from that withered rose
Mounted in antlers, up past the first morning
Glory's grasp of lightning rod,
Labor, cost, frostbite, bedazzlement,
Down to the last friend's guitar and stories,
Name called in sleep, fingers unclenching
In a long bath, its tepid amber inch
And dry bouquet—the future, gentlemen!

Tomorrow's cabin, who knows where, will seem
A shade sobered, abler to comprehend
How much, how little it takes to be thought worth
Crossing the threshold of, a place to dwell,
Will suffer once again the flashlight painless
Piercing of your dream, beam upon beam,

And its old boards before they turn to earth
Drink the mirage, the dreamer's volatile
Here all would have been well.

7
Sit then, draped in a sheet whose snowy folds
Darken in patches as when summer comes
And sun goes round and round the melting mountain.
Smiling debonair

You maybe wait for some not seen till now
Aspect of yours to blaze from the alembic
While one of mine in robe and slippers cries
Ah stay! Thou art so fair!

Or else are smiling not to wince recalling
Locks the grave sprang open. Blind, untrimmed,
Sheeted with cold, such rot and tangle must
In time be our affair.

But should you smile as those who doubt the novice
Hands they entrust their beautiful heads to,
I want to show you how the clumsiest love
Transfigures if you let it, if you dare.

There was a day when beauty, death, and love
Were coiled together in one crowning glory.
Shears in hand, we parted the dark waves . . .
Look at me, dear one. There.

8
Geode, the troll's melon
Rind of crystals velvet smoke meat blue
Formed far away under fantastic
Pressures, then cloven in two
By the taciturn rock shop man, twins now forever

Will they hunger for each other
When one goes north and ones goes east?

I expect minerals never do.
Enough for them was a feast
Of flaws, the molten start and glacial sleep,
The parting kiss.

Still face to face in halfmoonlight
Sparkling comes easy to the Gemini.

Centimeters deep yawns the abyss.

9
Master of the ruined watercolor,
Citizen no less of the botched country
Where shots attain the eagle, and the grizzly
Dies for pressing people to his heart,

Truster, like me, of who (invoked by neither)
Hovered near the final evening's taper,
Held his breath to read his flickering nature
By our light, then left us in the dark,

Take these verses, call them today's flower,
Cluster a rained-in pupil might have scissored.
They too have suffered in the realm of hazard.
Sorry things all. Accepting them's the art.

THE BLACK MESA

So much is parchment where I gloom,
Character still sharp enough to prick
Into the hide my igneous
Old spells and canticles of doom.
The things that shape a person! Peace.
Depth therapy in early stages crowned
One fuming anchorite with river stones.

Remember, though, how in *Thaïs*
The desert father falls for the land's lie—
That "grande horizontale" (blown shawls
Shining and raveling to this day
Above erosions in her pot of rouge)
Whom any crossing cloud turns dim,
Ascetic, otherworldly, lost to him.

By way of you a thousand human
Frailties found in me their last refuge.
The turquoise lodged for good one night
In a crevice where the young blood drummed.
Discharge, salvo, sulfur ringed me round
Below the waist. I knew thirst. Dawns,
The viceroy's eagle glittered like a gnat.

Sieges like that come late and end
Soon. And we are friends now? Funny friends.
Glaringly over years you knit
A wild green lap robe I shake off in tears.
I steal past him who next reclaims you, keep
Our hushed appointments, grain by grain . . .
Dust of my dust, when will it all be plain?

UNDER LIBRA: WEIGHTS AND MEASURES

for David McIntosh

The stones of spring,
Stale rolls or pellets rather, rounded
By a gorgon's fingers, swept to the floor,

Dragged south in crushing folds,
Long dirty tablecloth of ice,
Her feast ended, her intimates dispersed

Where certain curious formations
Dwindle in the red wind like ice in tea,
These stones, these poor scarred loaves

Lichen-crusted mould-gray or burnt orange
Stop doors and rest on manuscripts.
Backbreaking it was to haul them home.

Home. That winter's terrible storms,
Apartment shivering, whistling through its teeth,
Throb of a furnace fit to burst—

To go in the small hours from room to room
Stumbling onto their drugged stubborn sleep.

The heaviest dream
Gets told to the sunrise. The ditch
Hides its rapid and self-seeking nature

Beneath a blown glass simulacrum.
Mist and fire, tomorrow's opal
Defying gravity, inspiring it,

The sun will float across thin ice
To where two swans are dozing, swansdown quilts
Drawn over heads, feet tucked on top,

And snow be light as plumage upon theirs.
Paper windflowers like things possessed
Will dance upon Angel Ortiz

Leaving whose raw grave in the churchyard
The peacock, blue snake-neck zigzag
Through biscuit everlastings twice its height,

Will pass the shower window and not scream
Inward at a nude gone up in steam.

There then, his peacock
Past, the dreamer dries and gazes
Into the dormant crystal of himself,

A presence oval, vitrified—
That without warning thaws, trickles, and burns!
Frightened he looks away. He learns

To live whole days in another
Tense, avoid the bathroom scales or merely
Sing them. Wipe lather from his lip. Dress. Drive

Until the trees have leaves again
And the tanner's colors change to those of the mint,
Copper, silver, green

Engraved by summer's light, by spring's.
The riverbend's great horseshoe print
Where time turned round at last, drew rein,

Glints through a windshield blazing dust and wings,
Scum of the earth rebuffed upon the pane.

Under Libra: Weights and Measures

Warm afternoons
In his son's truck, Angel, both quick and dead,
Awaited judgment and suspended it.

His right side like a thing possessed
Danced, light birdclaw fast upon the guest.
The left had long let go—its tear

Oozed as from stone. It seemed
Both sides of the old character knew best.
In, out the unhinged doors

White coma'd spores were drifting, shining.
Flies lit, cudgeled quarter-carat wits,
Then washed their wings of him.

Blanca, too, who used to leap
Reeking of rain, licking his face like fire,
Lay back. Her coat caked red and speaking eyes

Clear as the baby's or the priest's
Wondered could he last another night.

For see, by dusk
A crescent jaw, a sudden frost of stubble
Yesterday's Gem will float across,

Enters the rear-view mirror. There was one
Direction only, after all?
How many more nights will that double-headed

Friend woven, wings outspread,
Into the dreamer's blanket keep him warm?
Here now's a little mesa set for two—

Over purple places, intimate
Twinklings, early stones, wide open spaces,
And soon on the horizon the "necklace of death"

Los Alamos' lights where wizards stay up late
(Stay in the car, forget the gate)
To save the world or end it, time will tell

—Mentioned for what it's worth in hopes
Of giving weight to—Brr! It's freezing!

Clay room. Firelight.
No measures taken, no words weighed—
As next morning, pen in hand, the whole

House sown by the prism on the sill
With arcs of spectral seed, a peacock's tail—
Or ten years from next morning, pen in hand,

Looking through saltwater, through flames,
Enkindlings of an absent *I* and *you,*
Live, spitting pronouns, sparks that flew

And were translated into windiest
Esperanto, zero tongue of powers
Diplomatic around 1 a.m.'s

Undripping centerpiece, the Swan . . .
Days were coming when the real thing
No longer shrugged a wing, dipping its mask

Where any surface thawed and burned.
One learned. The heavy stones of spring.
These autumn feathers. Learned.

KOMBOLOI

the Greek "worry-beads"

Begin. Carnation underfoot, tea splashing stars
Onto this mottled slab, amber coherences,

Unmatched string of the habitué
Told and retold, rubbed lucid, quick with scenes . . .

That face—fire-slitted fur, whip fury, slate iced over!
Click. An early life. The warrior's

Came late, enchanted brief. Then, gem on brow
And far-eyed peregrine on wrist,

One life in profile brushed so fine
You felt no single stroke until the last of thousands.

All that while, the bed had flowed, divided,
Deepened and sung in sparkling attacks

None but whose woman brought her warm specific,
Her tongue unspeakable. Click. Taxis

Yoked together floors below were making
Summer hell. Yet from her pupil streamed

Radii such as gall the ferry's shadow
Plunging like my pen past shoals of shilly-shally

Into fathomless gentian. Or into
Some thinnest "shade" of blue

Juniper berries fallen on this far bank
Of now no river. Wingbeats echo where its ghost

Forks. Focus the half mile down
Upon snapped golds—if not a corn plantation

Then a small ill-strung harp which dead hands pluck
And pluck. No sound. No issue. The wheel

Founders in red rainwater, soul inchdeep in pain,
Charred spokesman of reflections grimly

Sanguine with siftings from the great
Cracked hourglass. Click. Will . . . ? Click.

Will second wind come even to the runners
Out of time? These beads—O marble counter—Done.

STRATO IN PLASTER

στῆθος μάρμαρο καὶ καρδιὰ πατάτα

Out of the blue, in plaster from wrist to bicep
Somebody opens a beer, pretending to be
My friend Strato. Years or minutes—which?—
Have passed since we last looked upon each other.
He's in town for his sister's wedding
To this elderly thin-lipped sonofabitch
Who gets the house for dowry—enough to make
A brother break with the entire family.
Considering it, his eyes fairly cross
With self-importance. That, I recognize.

Here at hand is a postcard Chester sent
Of the Apollo at Olympia,
Its message *Strato as he used to be.*
Joy breeds in the beautiful blind gaze,
The marble mouth and breastbone. I look hard
At both the god and him. (He loves attention
Like gods and children, and he lifts his glass.)
Those extra kilos, that moustache,
Lies found out and letters left unanswered
Just won't do. It makes him burst out laughing,
Curiously happy, flecked with foam.

At present he is living far from home,
Builder by day and autocrat by dark,
Athenian among peasants. Fine Athenian
Whose wife learns acquiesence blow by blow.
That strikes a nerve. "I haven't married her!
Am I a fool to marry before thirty?
Who trusts a woman anyhow?
The nurse that set my elbow, filthy crone,
I cried out, it hurt so—but did she care?"
He goes on quickly, looking proud:

"I'm full of spite. Remember what you wrote
In answer to my asking for a loan?
I tore up your address—though you were right!—
Then sold the cufflinks and the black trenchcoat."

Now that he wants to go to El Dorado
His brother there has given up urging him.
"OK. I fuck his Virgin.
Bad son, bad father, and bad friend to you,
I might as well be a bad brother, too."
The little boy is three and "delicate"
But still "a devil, full of fight!"
My guest drinks up. Twin jewels unsold somehow,
His eyes are sparkling with delight.

Three winters, playing backgammon
At the café for stakes that pierce the heart,
One cigarette or dram of burning mud,
And never losing ("dice are in my blood")—
Marika sleeping, her cheeks ice,
Where oil smoke sickens and a chicken's cough
Wakes the child who dashes to the floor
Any red elixir *he* might pour—

Three winters. Trowels of frigid white
Choke the sugar-celled original
That once stayed warm all night with its own sun.
The god in him is a remembered one.
Inflexibility through which twinges shoot
Like stars, the fracture's too complex,
Too long unmended, for us to be friends.
I, he hazards, have made other friends.
The more reason, then, to part like friends.

Today at least a cloud of rice and petals
Aimed at others will envelop him.

Risen, he wonders—almost saying what.
I take his swollen hand in both of mine.

225

Strato in Plaster

No syllable of certain grand tirades
One spent the worse part of a fall composing,
Merely that word in common use
Which means both *foolishness* and *self-abuse*
Coming to mind, I smile:
Was the break caused by too much malakía?
Strato's answer is a final burst
Of laughter: "No such luck!
One day like this the scaffold gave beneath me.
I felt no pain at first."

UP AND DOWN

> "The heart that leaps to the invitation of sparkling
> appearances is the heart that would itself perform
> as handsomely."
>
> John H. Finley, Jr., *Four Stages of Greek Thought*

I. SNOW KING CHAIR LIFT

Prey swooped up, the iron love seat shudders
Onward into its acrophilic trance.
What folly has possessed us? Ambulance!
Give me your hand, try thinking of those others'

Unhurt return by twos from June's immense
Sunbeamed ark with such transfigured faces,
We sought admission on the shaky basis
That some good follows from experience

Of anything or leaving it behind,
As now, each urchin street and park sent sprawling
By the mountain's foot—why, this is fun, appalling
Bungalows, goodbye! dark frames of mind,

Whatever's settled into, comfort, despair,
Sin, expectation, apathy, the past,
Rigid interiors that will not outlast
Their decorator or their millionaire,

Groaning of board and bed of ruses, oh
I've had it up to here, fiftieth story
Glass maze, ice cube, daybreak's inflammatory
Montage subsiding into vertigo

Till, with their elevations all on file,
Joys, now demolished, that I used to live in,
This afternoon I swear halfway to heaven
None housed me—no, not style itself—in style.

Up and Down

Risen this far, your ex-materialist
Signs an impetuous long lease on views
Of several states and skies of several blues
Promptly dismantled by the mover mist

—What's going on? Loud ceiling shaken, brute
Maker of scenes in lightning spurt on spurt—
How did those others, how shall we avert
Illuminations that electrocute!

Except that suddenly the danger's gone.
Huge cloudscapes hang in the sun's antechamber.
Somebody takes our picture, calls a number.
We've done it. Reached the heights and quit our throne.

While knowing better, now, than to repeat
Our sole anabasis, unless in rhyme,
I love that funny snapshot from a time
When we still thought we were each other's meat.

The very great or very fatuous
Complicate the pinnacles they reach,
Plant banners, carve initials, end a speech,
"My fellow Texans, let us pray . . ." Not us.

You merely said you liked it in that chill
Lighthearted atmosphere (a crow for witness)
And I, that words profaned the driven whiteness
Of a new leaf. The rest was all downhill.

Au fond each summit is a cul-de-sac.
That day at least by not unprecedented
Foresight, a Cozy Cabin had been rented.
Before I led you to the next chair back

And made my crude but educated guess
At why the wind was laying hands on you
(Something I no longer think to do)
We gazed our little fills at boundlessness.

2. THE EMERALD

Hearing that on Sunday I would leave,
My mother asked if we might drive downtown.
Why certainly—off with my dressing gown!
The weather had turned fair. *We* were alive.

Only the gentle General she married
Late, for both an old way out of harm's,
Fought for breath, surrendered in her arms,
With military honors now lay buried.

That week the arcana of his medicine chest
Had been disposed of, and his clothes. Gold belt
Buckle and the letter from President Roosevelt
Went to an unknown grandchild in the West.

Downtown, his widow raised her parasol
Against the Lenten sun's not yet detectable
Malignant atomies which an electric needle
Unfreckles from her soft white skin each fall.

Hence too her chiffon scarf, pale violet,
And spangle-paste dark glasses. Each spring we number
The new dead. Above ground, who can remember
Her as she once was? Even I forget,

Fail to attend her, seem impervious . . .
Meanwhile we have made through a dense shimmy
Of parked cars burnished by the midday chamois
For Mutual Trust. Here cool gloom welcomes us,

And all, director, guard, quite palpably
Adore her. Spinster tellers one by one
Darting from cages, sniffling to meet her son,
Think of her having a son—! She holds the key

Up and Down

Whereby palatial bronze gates shut like jaws
On our descent into this inmost vault.
The keeper bends his baldness to consult,
Brings a tin box painted mud-brown, withdraws.

She opens it. Security. Will. Deed.
Rummages further. Rustle of tissue, a sprung
Lid. Her face gone queerly lit, fair, young,
Like faces of our dear ones who have died.

No rhinestone now, no dilute amethyst,
But of the first water, linking star to pang,
Teardrop to fire, my father's kisses hang
In lipless concentration round her wrist.

Gray are these temple-drummers who once more
Would rouse her, girl-bride jeweled in his grave.
Instead, she next picks out a ring. "He gave
Me this when you were born. Here, take it for—

For when you marry. For your bride. It's yours."
A den of greenest light, it grows, shrinks, glows,
Hermetic stanza bedded in the prose
Of the last thirty semiprecious years.

I do not tell her, it would sound theatrical,
Indeed this green room's mine, my very life.
We are each other's; there will be no wife;
The little feet that patter here are metrical.

But onto her worn knuckle slip the ring.
Wear it for me, I silently entreat,
Until—until the time comes. Our eyes meet.
The world beneath the world is brightening.

DREAMS ABOUT CLOTHES

for John and Anne Hollander

In some, the man they made
Penetrates the sunlit fitting room,
Once more deciding among bolts of dark.
The tailor kneels to take his measure.
Soon a finished suit will be laid out
By his valet, for him to change into.
Change of clothes? The very clothes of change!
Unchecked blazers women flutter round,
Green coverts, midnight blues . . .
My left hand a pincushion, I dispose,
Till morning, of whole closets full of clues.

What ought I in fact to do with them?
Give away suits worn six, eight times?
Take them to the shrink until they fit?
Have them mothproofed at least
(Arturo's Valet Service, one block East,
Picks up, delivers)—or just let them be,
Still holding sway above me, Harvard Law's
Loyal sons of '00 hanging by claws
On their slow shuttle to the sea.

Sure enough, a waterfront
Glides into place on small, oiled waves.
Taverns are glittering and the heavens have cleared.
(Far inland lie the crossroads,
Oxcart overturned, graybeard
Lamented by his slaves.)
From whom did I inherit these shirtsleeves
And ancient, sexy jeans?
Fingers of a woman I am with
Tease through holes made by the myth.
Bad music starts in 6/8 time.
I order drinks and dinners. I'm

Being taken, her smile means,
Once more to the cleaners.

Sleeping clean through those August afternoons
Whose Prospero, on shuttles quick as play,
Was weaving rainy spells—
Warp of physics, woof of whim;
Feeling him under some new pressure thunder
Forth in loud black surges to outsweat
Until the lightning twinkling of an eye
Dissolved his corporation,
The tempest used to be my cup of tea.
(Come in, Mme de Garments called,
You'll be soaked to the skin! I never woke.)
Relief poured through me shining wet,
Lining of purest silver.

But now, his baby face unlined and bald,
The old-clothes man comes down the street,
Singing the little song he sings.
His overcoat is all humped up in back
To hide his powerful wings.
Snow melts at the touch of his bare feet.
He passes me unseeing, yet how much
Of mine's already in his sack!

Tell me something, Art.
You know what it's like
Awake in your dry hell
Of volatile synthetic solvents.
Won't you help us brave the elements
Once more, of terror, anger, love?
Seeing there's no end to wear and tear
Upon the lawless heart,
Won't you as well forgive
Whoever settles for the immaterial?
Don't you care how we live?

FLÈCHE D'OR

Windowglass, warmed plush, a sneeze
Deflected by the miracle
Into euphoria's
Authoritative gliding forth,
The riddle of the rails
Vitally unmoved in flight
However fast
I run racing that arrow
Lodged in my brain
Down the board platform beyond hurt or hope
Once more, once more
My life ended, having not,
Veils lifted, words from the page
Come to my senses
Eased of that last arrivederci deep
In book or view, my own
Fleet profile calmer catapulted due
North a pane floats off, desire sinks
Red upon piercing stubble—"Traveler,
Turn back!" the tracks
Outcry, din flash fade, done,
Over forever, done I say, now yet
Might somebody
Seeing it all (for once not I or I)
Judge us wisely in whose heart of
Hearts the parallels
Meet and nothing lasts and nothing ends

DAYS OF 1971

Fallen from the clouds, well-met.
This way to the limousine.
How are things? Don't tell me yet!
Have a Gauloise first, I mean.

Matches now, did I forget—
With a flourish and no word
Out came the sentry-silhouette
Black against a big, flame-feathered bird,

Emblem of your "new" regime
Held, for its repressive ways,
In pretty general disesteem

Which to share just then was hard,
Borne up so far on a strategic blaze
Struck by you, and quite off guard.

In Paris you remark each small
Caged creature, marmoset, bat, newt, for sale;
Also the sparkling gutters, and the smelly
Seine this afternoon when we embark.

And the Bateau Mouche is spoiled by a party of cripples.
Look at what's left of that young fellow strapped
Into his wheelchair. How you pity him!
The city ripples, your eyes sicken and swim.

The boy includes you in his sightseeing,
Nodding sociably as if who of us
Here below were more than half a man.

There goes the Louvre, its Egyptian wing
Dense with basalt limbs and heads to use
Only as one's imagination can.

Can-can from last night's *Orphée aux Enfers*
Since daybreak you've been whistling till I wince.
Well, you were a handsome devil once.
Take the wheel. You're still a fair chauffeur.

Our trip. I'd pictured it another way—
Asthmatic pilgrim and his "nun of speed,"
In either mind a music spun of need . . .
That last turnoff went to Illiers.

Proust's Law (are you listening?) is twofold:
(a) What least thing our self-love longs for most
Others instinctively withhold;

(b) Only when time has slain desire
Is his wish granted to a smiling ghost
Neither harmed nor warmed, now, by the fire.

Stephen in the Pyrenees—our first
Real stop. You promptly got a stomachache.
Days of groans and grimaces interspersed
With marathon slumbers. Evenings, you'd wake

And stagger forth to find us talking. Not
Still about poetry! Alas . . .
So bottles were produced, and something hot.
The jokes you told translated, more or less.

Predictably departure cured you. Stephen
Investing me with a Basque walking stick,
"How much further, James, will you be driven?"

He didn't ask. He stood there, thin, pale, kind
As candlelight. Ah, what if *I* took sick?
You raced the motor, having read my mind.

Days of 1971

Sucked by haste into the car,
Pressing his frantic buzzer, Bee!
Suppose he stings—why such hilarity?
These things occur.

Get rid of him at once
While we can! His wrath
Is almost human, the windshield's warpath
Dins with a song and dance

In one respect unlike our own:
Readily let out into the open.
There. Good creature, also he had known
The cost of self-as-weapon;

Venom unspent, barb idle, knows
Where they led now—thyme, lavender, musk-rose,

Toulouse, Toulon, the border. Driven?
At ease, rather, among fleeting scenes.
The O L I V E T T I signs
Whizz by, and azure Lombardy is given

Back, as the Virgin of Officialdom
Severely draped twists on her throne to peek
At the forbidden crags of kingdom come
Before resuming her deft hunt and peck.

One V sticks. Venice. Its vertiginous pastry
Maze we scurry through like mice and will
Never see the likes of in our lives.

It is too pink, white, stale to taste,
Crumbling in the gleam of slimy knives.
Have your cake and eat it? Take the wheel.

Wait—now where are we? Who is everyone?
Well, that's a Princess, that's the butler . . . no,
Probably by now the butler's son.
We were stopping till tomorrow with Umberto

Among trompe l'oeil, old volumes, photographs
Of faded people wearing crowns and stars.
Welcome to the Time Machine, he laughed
Leaning on us both up its cold stairs.

At table the others recalled phrases from
Homer and Sappho, and you seemed to brighten.
Your sheets would entertain the "priest" that night
(Dish of embers in a wooden frame)

And eyes glaze on the bedside book, remote
But near, pristine but mildewed, which I wrote.

Take the wheel. San Zeno will survive
Whether or not visited.
Power is knowledge in your head.
(Sorry, I must have been thinking aloud. Drive, drive.)

Time and again the novel I began
Took aim at that unwritten part
In which the hero, named Sebastian,
Came to his senses through a work of art.

O book of hours, those last
Illuminated castles built
In air, O chariot-motif

Bearing down a margin good as gilt
Past fields of ever purer leaf
Its burning rubric, to get nowhere fast . . .

Days of 1971

The road stopped where a Greek mountain fell
Early that week. Backed-up cars glared in the dusk.
Night fell next, and still five stupid slack-
Jawed ferries hadn't got their fill of us.

Tempers shortened. One self-righteous truck
Knocked the shit out of a eucalyptus
Whose whitewashed trunk lay twitching brokenly—
Nijinsky in *Petrouchka*—on the quai.

Later, past caring, packed like sheep,
Some may have felt the breathless lounge redeemed
By a transistor singing to the doomed

At last in their own tongue. You fell asleep
Life-sentenced to the honey-cell of song,
Harsh melisma, torturous diphthong.

Strato, each year's poem
Says goodbye to you.
Again, though, we've come through
Without losing temper or face.

If care rumpled your face
The other day in Rome,
Tonight just dump my suitcase
Inside the door and make a dash for home

While I unpack what we saw made
At Murano, and you gave to me—
Two ounces of white heat
Twirled and tweezered into shape,

Ecco! another fanciful
Little horse, still blushing, set to cool.

THE VICTOR DOG

for Elizabeth Bishop

Bix to Buxtehude to Boulez,
The little white dog on the Victor label
Listens long and hard as he is able.
It's all in a day's work, whatever plays.

From judgment, it would seem, he has refrained.
He even listens earnestly to Bloch,
Then builds a church upon our acid rock.
He's man's—no—he's the Leiermann's best friend,

Or would be if hearing and listening were the same.
Does he hear? I fancy he rather smells
Those lemon-gold arpeggios in Ravel's
"Les jets d'eau du palais de ceux qui s'aiment."

He ponders the Schumann Concerto's tall willow hit
By lightning, and stays put. When he surmises
Through one of Bach's eternal boxwood mazes
The oboe pungent as a bitch in heat,

Or when the calypso decants its raw bay rum
Or the moon in *Wozzeck* reddens ripe for murder,
He doesn't sneeze or howl; just listens harder.
Adamant needles bear down on him from

Whirling of outer space, too black, too near—
But he was taught as a puppy not to flinch,
Much less to imitate his bête noire Blanche
Who barked, fat foolish creature, at King Lear.

Still others fought in the road's filth over Jezebel,
Slavered on hearths of horned and pelted barons.
His forebears lacked, to say the least, forbearance.
Can nature change in him? Nothing's impossible.

The Victor Dog

The last chord fades. The night is cold and fine.
His master's voice rasps through the grooves' bare groves.
Obediently, in silence like the grave's
He sleeps there on the still-warm gramophone

Only to dream he is at the première of a Handel
Opera long thought lost—*Il Cane Minore*.
Its allegorical subject is his story!
A little dog revolving round a spindle

Gives rise to harmonies beyond belief,
A cast of stars. . . . Is there in Victor's heart
No honey for the vanquished? Art is art.
The life it asks of us is a dog's life.

SYRINX

Bug, flower, bird on slipware fired and fluted,
The summer day breaks everywhere at once.

Worn is the green of things that have known dawns
Before this, and the darkness before them.

Among the wreckage, bent in Christian weeds,
Illiterate—X my mark—I tremble, still

A thinking reed. Who puts his mouth to me
Draws out the scale of love and dread—

O ramify, sole antidote! Foxglove
Each year, cloud, hornet, fatal growths

Proliferating by metastasis
Rooted their total in the gliding stream.

Some formula not relevant any more
To flower children might express it yet

Like

$$\sqrt{\left(\frac{x}{y}\right)^{n}} = 1$$

—Or equals zero, one forgets—

The y standing for you, dear friend, at least
Until that hour he reaches for me, then

Leaves me cold, the great god Pain,
Letting me slide back into my scarred case

Whose silvery breath-tarnished tones
No longer rivet bone and star in place

Syrinx

Or keep from shriveling, leather round a stone,
The sunbather's precocious apricot

Or stop the four winds racing overhead

Nought

Waste   Eased

Sought

From Divine Comedies (1976)

THE KIMONO

When I returned from lovers' lane
My hair was white as snow.
Joy, incomprehension, pain
I'd seen like seasons come and go.
How I got home again
Frozen half dead, perhaps you know.

You hide a smile and quote a text:
Desires ungratified
Persist from one life to the next.
Hearths we strip ourselves beside
Long, long ago were x'd
On blueprints of "consuming pride."

Times out of mind, the bubble-gleam
To our charred level drew
April back. A sudden beam . . .
—Keep talking while I change into
The pattern of a stream
Bordered with rushes white on blue.

McKANE'S FALLS

The great cold shoulders bared,
The last great masts grown rich with moss, the slow-to-topple
Pilings, amassings of a shadily

Conservative nature—Balzac alone
Could have "done" this old salon,
Its airs, its tediums. The more astounding, then,

To be led by laughter out onto the sunny balcony
Where somebody quite dashing for a change
Ran on about banks broken and weights lifted,

Dorsals, laterals, pure and simple
Ripplings of a soul
—Lost, mon père? Well . . . savable, who knows?

They knew. The two dirt-caked prospectors
Rubbed their eyes and squatted within earshot:
A Yankee ornery enough to seek

Unfluctuating values, and a meek
Rebel, an embittered dreamer
Out of Balzac. For what it was worth, God loved them—

His 12 oz. rainbow sizzled in their pan;
Next morning, the first nugget.
The creek, a crystal tendon strained,

Tossed on its couch, no longer freely associating
Hawk with trout, or cloud with pebble white as cloud.
Its mouth worked. The history began.

1

Since being gelded of my gold,
Gray moods, black moods come over me.
Where's my old sparkle? Of late
I've felt so rushed, so cold.

Am I riding for another fall?
Will I end up at the power station
On charges, a degenerate?
Have my spirit broken in a cell?

Must I grow broad- and dirty-minded
Serving a community, a nation
By now past anybody's power to shock?

Doctor of locks and dams, the delta's blinded,
The mudfish grins, how do I reach the sea?
Help me. No! Don't touch me! Let me be!

2

Time was, time was a handful of gold dust
Fought for like breath, though it was only time.
Grain by grain sifting to a slender waist
Inevitably, the climber gave
Up on those slopes so sheer they seemed concave.   ,

Here below, the campsite—second growth,
Charred beams, a skillet dew gnaws bottomless.
Of our two actors, which one surfaced then
In the casino mirrors of Cheyenne?
Why was his partner not apparent? Guess.

Listen. We must be near. And look, the currant
Berries—how their scarlets drip
Into clear conscience from a fingertip,
Or shrivel, tiny redskins, where next spring
Will rise big ghost-white scentless violets.

247

Senseless violence! Our quarrels, friend,
Have been, how shall I say,
Mortal as theirs, but less material.
You played your part in a Far Eastern theatre.
I stayed home with Balzac, and meditated.

Red shelter from the blizzard thought, bloodshed . . .
No hands are washed clean in the same stream twice.
And in the novel which was to have ended the *Comédie*
Little Hanno Nucingen is lost at sea,
A figure of angelic sacrifice.

3
Come live within me, said the waterfall.
There is a chamber of black stone
High and dry behind my stunning life.
Stay here a year or two, a year or ten,
Until you've heard it all,
The inside story deafening but true.

Or false—I'm not a fool.
Moments of truth are moments only,
Eyes burning on the brink of empty beds.
The years wink past, the current changes course.
Ruined by tin-pan blues
The golden voice turns gravelly and hoarse.

Now you've seen through me, sang the cataract,
A fraying force, but unafraid,
Plunge through my bath of plus and minus both,
Acid and base,
The mind that mirrors and the hands that act.
Enter this inmost space

Its lean illuminations decompose.
Sun's rose wash on the wall,
Moon clinging like the Perils of Pauline—
God knows I haven't failed her yet!
And yet how far away they seem, how small.
Get me by heart, my friend,

And then forget. Forgive
These bones their hollow end, this amulet
Its wearer who atones.
All things in time grow musical.
How can you live without me? While I live
Come live within me, said the waterfall.

CHIMES FOR YAHYA

1

Imperiously ringing, "Νὰ τὰ ποῦμε;
(Shall we tell it?)" two dressy little girls inquire.
They mean some chanted verse to do with Christmas
Which big homemade iron triangles
Drown out and a least coin silences
But oh hell not at seven in the morning
If you please! and SLAM the frosted glass
Spares me their tidings and themselves
Further inspection of the foreigner
Grizzled and growling in his flannel robe.
All day children will be prowling loose
Eager to tell, tell, tell what the angel said.
So, having gagged the mechanism with a towel,
Washed hands and face, put on the kettle—
But bells keep ringing in my head.
Downhill too, where priests pace in black dresses,
Chignons and hats, like Chekhov's governesses,
Their toy church on a whole block of bare earth
In central Athens (what it must be worth!)
Clangs like a locomotive—well, good lord,
Why not? Tomorrow's Christmas. All aboard.

2

Another memory of Mademoiselle.
We're in a Pullman going South for Christmas,
She in the lower berth, I in the upper
As befits whatever station we pass through.
Lanterns finger our compartment walls.
At one stop, slipping down into her dream
I lift the blind an inch. Outside, some blanketed
Black figures from a crèche, part king,
Part shepherd and part donkey, stamp and steam
Gliding from sight as rapturous bells ring.
Mummy and Daddy have gone ahead by sleigh
Packard piled with gifts I know too well.
Night after autumn night, Mademoiselle

250

Yielding to endearments, bringing down
From the attic, lion by tiger, acrobat by clown,
Tamer with her little whips and hoops,
The very circus of my wildest hopes,
I've seen it, memorized it all. *Choo-choo*
Goes the train towards the déjà-vu.
Christmas morning, in a Mandarin suit—
Pigtail and fan, and pipe already staled
By the imaginary stuff inhaled—
I mimed astonishment, and who was fooled?
The treasure lay outspread beneath the tree.
Pitiful, its delusive novelty:
A present far behind me, in a sense.
And this has been a problem ever since.

3
While I carry tea up to the terrace
—The day is ravishingly mild and fair—
Thirty years pass. My train of thought
Stalls near a certain tunnel's end—despair
Lit by far-off daylight . . . Isfahan.
Change of scene that might, I thought, be tried
First, instead of outright suicide.
(Looked back on now, what caused my sufferings?
Mere thwarted passion—commonest of things.)
I had been shown into a freezing room
Belonging to a man I didn't know.
"What does that matter? Simply go,"
The friend of friends had said. (These friends of friends
Were better company, that year, than real ones.)
Surrendering his letter with my shoes,
Was taking what cold comfort one can take
When one's heart is breaking, on the carpet.
The carpet? Carpet overlapping carpet,
Threadbare, opulent. Enormous carpet-
Covered cushions. On the wall a carpet
Portrait of an old forbidding man
Correct in carpet cutaway, tarboosh
And deep white pile moustache: my host's grandfather,

As I would learn, who founded the carpet works.
Rose trees in such bloom they looked unreal
(Odorless also, or had I caught cold?)
Stood in the four corners. Nearby squatted
A brazier wheezing like a bronchitic old
Bulldog, ash-white, garnet-eyed.
Smoke curled, cardings from the comb of light,
Between me and a courtyard still in shadow.
A well. A flowering tree. One tethered goat,
Her face both smug and martyred, giving suck
To a white puppy's warm, incarnate mess
Of instincts only the pure in heart confess.
Back and forth, grimly eyebrowed under shawls,
Humans passed jacketed in sheepskin.
Was that a gentle summons from within?
The person entering, as I made to rise,
Sketched a rapid unrepeatable gesture
Perfectly explicit. "I," it said,
"Am an old retainer. By these eyes
I would not have you see me otherwise—
Unless you cared to sample my poor graces,
Lampblack and henna, on a hazier basis,"
Kneeling, he arranges full black trousers
To hide his striped socks full of holes,
And fusses with the kettle on the coals.

4
"Ah, you have met Hussein," the gentle voice
Just heard says at my shoulder. There
In your corduroy jumpsuit, knotting a foulard
Of camouflage greens-and-browns, you are. You are
No older or younger than I've pictured you,
No handsomer, no simpler—only kinder.
Lover, warrior, invalid and sage,
Amused, unenvious of one another,
Meet in your face. Hussein pours cups too full.
"Our friend is fidgeting. Time for his pipe.
You don't object? I used to smoke myself,
Before my father died and I became

252

What—the prince? the chieftain of our tribe?
We're smiling but it's serious. One belongs
To the working class of prince. The feuds alone—
Tribesmen at one's gate from miles away,
Needing a doctor or a judgment. Summers, though,
We all live *their* life, high in the foothills,
A world you wouldn't dream. Perhaps one day . . . "
Meanwhile Hussein, positioning the tar
Pearl upon his cloudy blue-green globe,
Applies a coal, is sucking peacefully
At the long polished stem. Peculiar
Sweetness—so I *can* smell—fills the air.
As for the roses, you apologize,
"Roses in Isfahan don't bloom till May.
These are imitation, from Times Square."

5
You kept me by you all that day.
I never had to think why I was there.
Figures materialized, obeyed, unraveled.
One young man brought you his smooth breast
Like an heirloom to unwrap, to probe and dress.
Hussein brought omelets, brandy, cake, fruit, lamb.
A barber shaved you. A tall blonde from Berkeley,
Gloria, doing fieldwork in the tribe,
Got asked back that evening for dinner.
After she left: "Or don't you like
The company of your compatriots?"
I liked whatever you would ask me to,
Wanted to get so many lines a week
Of you by heart. Would want tomorrow
When, to senses sharpened by the pipe
Shared with Hussein once you had gone to bed,
Jets of rigid color—the great mosque—
Rose from a pure white carpet, snowlight flowing
Through every vein and duct, would want to spend
One lifetime there as a divinity
Student niched in shallowest faience,
Pilaf steaming while the slow air

Dried his turban's green outfloating prayer.
Had there perhaps already been
Lives at your side? A paperback I read
Compares the soul to a skimmed stone
Touching the waters of the world at points
Along a curve—Atlantis, Rome, Versailles—
Where friends arrange to be reborn together.
Absurd? No more than Freud or Chemistry
To explain the joy, the jolt that had set wheels
Rolling toward some vapor-tasseled view
—And, incidentally, away from you.

6
Not a year later, ink-blue stains
Would spell the worst—a "letter" of Hussein's:

A boyhood skirmish, a (word blotted) slug
Lodged in your skull, which must . . . which finally must . . .

Prince, that the perennial gift (remember)
Unroll another time beneath your feet,

That, red with liability to bloom
And blow, the rose abstainer of your loom

Quicken a pattern ever incomplete,
Dear prince in whom I put my trust,

Away with pipe and ember,
The real thing's dark and malleable drug;

Withdrawal rendering, as we know, more strict
Our buried craving for the habit kicked.

7
Dinner was over. Hussein spoke in your ear.
You nodded him away. We drained our beer.
Gloria went right on theorizing

About "relationships within the tribe"
I now appeared to be a member of—
Dressed by you in the black ballooning trousers,
White vest, coarse sherbet-colored shirt
And brimless derby hat your people wore.
(I wore them here once during Carnival
With burnt cork eyebrows. Nobody was fooled.)
Time for a highball? But a piercing scream
Somewhere in the household interrupted
Our flow of spirits. What on earth . . .?
"Ah, it's too tiresome," you sighed.
"These mountain women *will* give birth
Under one's roof. They wait until their labor's
So far advanced we've no way to prepare—"
The girl from Berkeley lit up like a flare:
"In two whole years I've—oh I've told and told you—
Never seen a childbirth! Can't we just—"
You shook your head. "Ah no. The stranger
Brings bad luck, we think. Best let her be.
A doctor? No. Hussein knows an old woman.
He's gone to fetch her." "But I must, must, must!
Think of my thesis, Yahya, let me please!"
Gloria had risen to her knees.
Counterpoint of screams and argument
Making you disdainfully relent,
"All right. But quietly. Into your coats."
And into the cold courtyard black with goats.

Across, a glimmering shutter stood ajar.
Come-and-go of oil lamps, moans and shadows.
As far as we could tell on tiptoe, there
In the small room's dissolving shabbiness
Lay this veiled figure writhing on a carpet.
Gloria found the bench, I climbed beside her.
Elbows on sill, we presently were staring
While you chuckled back against the wall,
Staring like solemn oxen from a stall
Upon the mystery. "Wow," breathed Gloria,
"Smell that smell. They gave her opium."

255

Women were chanting. The midwife had come.
Maternal invocations and convulsions
Reaching a pitch—did I detect
In all that pain an element of play?
You also seemed convulsed, with laughter, why?—
Reaching a pitch, an infant's feeble cry
From underneath dark swathings clove the night.
These totteringly picked themselves erect.
Made for Gloria. Into her credulous
Outstretched arms laid—*not* a wriggling white
Puppy! Horrors twinkled through the brain.
Then the proud mother bared her face: Hussein.

8
Cooling tea and clouding day . . .
Over the neighborhood prevailing
Bells, triangles, tuneless treble voices
Of children one imagines. Little boys
Whose rooster tessitura, plus ça change,
Will crow above the cradle of a son.
Little girls each with her Christmas doll
Like hens a china egg is slipped beneath.
Voices so familiar by now
It might as well be silence that I sit in,
Reliving romps with my animal nature. Its ecstasy
Knocking me over, off the leash at last
Or out of the manger at least; tongue, paw and pelt,
Loyal fearless heart—the vipers it saved us from;
Unlikeness to myself I knelt embracing.
Times, too, it turned on me, or on another—
Squawks, feathers—until the rolled-up *Times*
Imposed obedience. Now by its own scale
Older than I am, stodgy, apprehensive,
For all I know, of what must soon . . .
Yet trustful, setting blurred sights on me still.
What were five or six half playful bites?
Deep no doubt, but the pain so long forgiven
It might as well be pleasure I rise in,

9

Grazing music as I do so—my bells,
Silent all this while, my camel bells
From Isfahan. Their graduated brass
Pendant hangs on the awning-frame, discolored
Shades of dully wintering
Oleander. Verdigris on fingertip
And sleeve dew-wet, to make them ring
Together, reach down for the smallest. Shake.
A tingling spine of tone, or waterfall
Crashing pure and chill, bell within bell,
Upward to the ninth and mellowest,
Their changes mingle with the parish best,
Their told tale with the children's doggerel.

MANOS KARASTEFANÍS

Death took my father.
The same year (I was twelve)
Thanási's mother taught me
Heaven and hell.

None of my army buddies
Called me by name—
Just "Styles" or "Fashion Plate."
One friend I had, my body,

And, evenings at the gym
Contending with another,
Used it to isolate
Myself from him.

The doctor saved my knee.
You came to the clinic
Bringing *War and Peace*,
Better than any movie.

Why are you smiling?
I fought fair, I fought well,
Not hurting my opponent,
To win this black belt.

Why are you silent?
I've brought you a white cheese
From my island, and the sea's
Voice in a shell.

YÁNNINA

for Stephen Yenser

> "There lay the peninsula stretching far into the
> dark gray water, with its mosque, its cypress tufts
> and fortress walls; there was the city stretching far
> and wide along the water's edge; there was the fa-
> tal island, the closing scene of the history of the
> once all-powerful Ali."
>
> EDWARD LEAR

Somnambulists along the promenade
Have set up booths, their dreams:
Carpets, jewelry, kitchenware, halvah, shoes.
From a loudspeaker passionate lament
Mingles with the penny Jungle's roars and screams.
Tonight in the magician's tent
Next door a woman will be sawed in two,
But right now she's asleep, as who is not, as who . . .

An old Turk at the water's edge has laid
His weapons and himself down, sleeps
Undisturbed since, oh, 1913.
Nothing will surprise him should he wake,
Only how tall, how green the grass has grown
There by the dusty carpet of the lake
Sun beats, then sleepwalks down a vine-festooned arcade,
Giving himself away in golden heaps.

And in the dark gray water sleeps
One who said no to Ali. Kiosks all over town
Sell that postcard, "Kyra Frossíni's Drown,"
Showing her, eyeballs white as mothballs, trussed
Beneath the bulging moon of Ali's lust.
A devil (turban and moustache and sword)
Chucks the pious matron overboard—
Wait—Heaven help us—SPLASH!

Yánnina

The torch smokes on the prow. Too late.
(A picture deeply felt, if in technique slapdash.)
Wherefore the Lion of Epirus, feared
By Greek and Turk alike, tore his black beard
When to barred casements rose the song
Broken from bubbles rising all night long:
"A ton of sugar pour, oh pour into the lake
To sweeten it for poor, for poor Frossíni's sake."*

Awake? Her story's aftertaste
Varies according to the listener.
Friend, it's bitter coffee you prefer?
Brandy for me, and with a fine
White sandy bottom. Not among those braced
By action taken without comment, neat,
Here's how! Grounds of our footnote infiltrate the treat,
Mud-vile to your lips, crystal-sweet to mine.

Twilight at last. Enter the populace.
One little public garden must retrace
Long after school its childish X,
Two paths that cross and cross. The hollyhock, the rose,
Zinnia and marigold hear themselves named
And blush for form's sake, unashamed
Chorus out of *Ignoramus Rex*:
"What shall the heart learn, that already knows

Its place by water, and its time by sun?"
Mother wit fills the stately whispering sails
Of girls someone will board and marry. Who?
Look at those radiant young males.

*"Time was kind to the reputation of this woman who had been unfaithful to
her husband, vain, and grasping. She came to be regarded as a Christian martyr
and even as an early heroine in the struggle for Greek independence. She has
been celebrated in legend, in poetry, in popular songs and historical fiction, and
surrounded with the glamour which so often attaches to women whose love af-
fairs have been of an intense nature and have involved men of political or histor-
ical importance."

WILLIAM PLOMER, *The Diamond of Jannina*.

Their morning-glory nature neon blue
Wilts here on the provincial vine. Where did it lead,
The race, the radiance? To oblivion
Dissembled by a sac of sparse black seed.

Now under trees men with rush baskets sell
Crayfish tiny and scarlet as the sins
In any fin-de-siècle villanelle.
Tables fill up. A shadow play begins.
Painted, translucent cut-outs fill the screen.
It glows. His children by a jumping bean
Karaghiózi clobbers, baits the Turk,
Then all of them sing, dance, tell stories, go berzerk.

Tomorrow we shall cross the lake to see
The cottage tumbling down, where soldiers killed
Ali. Two rugless rooms. Cushions. Vitrines
In which, to this day, silks and bracelets swim.
Above, a painting hangs. It's him,
Ali. The end is near, he's sleeping between scenes
In a dark lady's lap. Vassilikí.
The mood is calm, the brushwork skilled

By contrast with Frossíni's mass-produced
Unsophisticated piece of goods.
The candle trembles in the watching god's
Hand—almost a love-death, höchste Lust!
Her drained, compliant features haunt
The waters there was never cause to drown her in.
Your grimiest ragamuffin comes to want
Two loves, two versions of the Feminine:

One virginal and tense, brief as a bubble,
One flesh and bone—gone up no less in smoke
Where giant spits revolving try their rusty treble,
Sheep's eyes pop, and death-wish ravens croak.

Remember, the Romantic's in full feather.
Byron has visited. He likes
The luxe, and overlooks the heads on pikes;
Finds Ali "very kind . . . indeed, a father . . ."★

Funny, that is how I think of Ali.
On the one hand, the power and the gory
Details, pigeon-blood rages and retali-
ations, gouts of fate that crust his story;
And on the other, charm, the whimsically
Meek brow, its motives all ab ulteriori,
The flower-blue gaze twining to choke proportion,
Having made one more pretty face's fortune.

A dove with Parkinson's disease
Selects *our* fortunes: TRAVEL AND GROW WISE
And A LOYAL FRIEND IS MORE THAN GOLD.
But, at the island monastery, eyes
Gouged long since to the gesso sockets will outstare
This or that old timer on his knees
Asking the candlelight for skill to hold
The figures flush against the screen's mild glare.

Ali, my father—both are dead.
In so many words, so many rhymes,
The brave old world sleeps. Are we what it dreams
And is a rude awakening overdue?
Not in Yánnina. To bed, to bed.
The Lion sets. The lights wink out along the lake.
Weeks later, in this study gone opaque,
They are relit. See through me. See me through.

★Letter to his mother, November 12, 1809. Plomer observes: ". . . even allow-
ing for Oriental effusiveness, it seems doubtful whether [Ali's] interest in Byron
was exactly as paternal as he pretended, for a father does not give his son sweets
twenty times a day and beg him to visit him at night. It is worth remarking that
Ali was a judge of character and a connoisseur of beauty, whether male or fe-
male, and that the like of Byron, and Byron at twenty one, is not often seen."

For partings hurt although we dip the pain
Into a glowing well—the pen I mean.
Living alone won't make some inmost face to shine
Maned with light, ember and anodyne,
Deep in a desktop burnished to its grain.
That the last hour be learned again
By riper selves, couldn't you doff this green
Incorruptible, the might-have-been,

And arm in arm with me dare the magician's tent?
It's hung with asterisks. A glittering death
Is hefted, swung. The victim smiles consent.
To a sharp intake of breath she comes apart
(Done by mirrors? Just one woman? Two?
A fight starts—in the provinces, one feels,
There's never that much else to do)
Then to a general exhalation heals

Like anybody's life, bubble and smoke
In afterthought, whose elements converge,
Glory of windless mornings that the barge
(Two barges, one reflected, a quicksilver joke)
Kept scissoring and mending as it steered
The old man outward and away,
Amber mouthpiece of a narghilé
Buried in his by then snow white beard.

VERSE FOR URANIA

Through the dimness, curtains drawn, eyes closed,
Where I am composing myself before tonight's excitement
(It's not quite five, yet outdoors the daylight
Will have begun to ripple and deepen like a pool)
Comes your mother's footstep, her voice softly,
Hesitantly calling. She'll have come upstairs
To borrow something for the evening, cups or chairs,
But it can't be urgent, and the footsteps fade
Before I've made my mind up, whether to answer.

Below, where you live, time will be standing cowed
Among the colors and appliances.
What passionate consumers you've become!
Second washing machine, giant second TV,
Hot saffron, pink, eyeshadow ultramarine—
Rooms like those ghostly ones behind the screen
With just the color tuned to Very Loud.
Your father's out in his new Silver Cloud
Delivering invitations. You've all been
Up since dawn—not you, of course, you're a baby,
But your mother and your sister. Between chores
Teasing each other's hair like sisters, touching
Rouged indexes to one another's cheek.
The lamb will have cooled nicely in its fat now,
Cake been iced to match the souvenir
Rosettes (two ribbons with your name and mine),
Whiskey and set-ups set up like tenpins.
According to tradition I'm affecting
Ignorance of, the post-baptismal party
Ought to be given by the godfather.
But this is your godfather speaking, calling halt.
I have already showered you with garments
Priced inversely to their tininess.
Have been shown rushes of what else my doom

Is to provide you with, world without end:
Music lessons from beyond the tomb,
Doll and dentist and dowry, the 3-D
Third television we attain so far
Exclusively in dreamland, where you are.
Would that *I* were. All too soon I'll place
Round your neck a golden chain and cross
Set with stones watery as the stars at noon;
And don't forget the fancy sheet you'll want
The moment you are lifted, born anew
Squalling and squirming out of the deep font,
While the priest lifts only his deep baritone
That makes the skull a vault of melismatic
Sparklings, and myself groan with your weight—
Renunciation of the vanities
In broken Byzantine on your behalf,
Or your father's flashbulbs popping, or your mother's eyes
Laughing to see salvation's gas inflate
Their fat peach-petal bébé-Michelin,
Not having made you, on me, a lighter burden.

Time drawing near, a clock that loses it
Tells me you must wake now, pagan still.
Slowly the day-glo minnow mobile twirls
Above you. Fin-glints ripple in the glass
Protecting an embroidery—your great-
Grandmother's? No one remembers. Appliquéd
On black: cross-section of a pomegranate,
Stem and all. The dull gold velvet rind
Full as a womb with flowers. Their faded silks entwine
The motto ΚΙ ΑΥΤΟ ΘΑ ΠΕΡΑΣΗ—This too will pass.

You're being named for yet another
Science whose elements cause vertigo
Even, I fancy, in the specialist.
A sleepless and unlettered urban glow

On everyone's horizon turns to gist
That rhetoric of starry beasts and gods
Whose figures, whose least phoneme made its fine
Point in the course of sweeping periods—
Each sentence thirty lives long, here below.
From out there notions may yet reach us, few
And far between as those first names we knew
Already without having to look up,
Children that we were, the Chair, the Cup,
But each night dimmer, children that we are,
Each night regressing, dumber by a star.
Still, fiction helps preserve them, those old truths
Our sleights have turned to fairy tales (or worse:
Look at—don't look at—your TV).
The storybooks you'll soon be reading me
About the skies abound with giants and dwarfs.
Think of the wealth of pre-Olympian
Amber washed up on the shores of Grimm—
The beanstalk's tenant-cyclops grown obese
On his own sons; the Bears and Berenice.
Or take those masterfully plotted high
Society conjunctions and epicycles
In a late fable like *The Wings of the Dove*.
Take, for that matter, my beanstalk couplet, above,
Where such considerations as rhyme and meter
Prevail, it might be felt, at the expense
Of meaning, but as well create, survive it;
For the first myth was Measure. Finally take
Any poor smalltown starstruck sense of "love
That makes the world go round"—see how the phrase
Stretches from Mystic to Mount Palomar
Back to those nights before the good old days,
Before the axle jumped its socket so
That genes in shock flashed on/off head to toe,
Before mill turned to maelstrom, and IBM
Wrenched from Pythagoras his diadem.

Adamant nights in which our wisest apes
Met on a cracked mud terrace not yet Ur
And with presumption more than amateur
Stared the random starlight into shapes.

Millennia their insight had to flee
Outward before the shaft it had become
Shot back through the planetarium
Cathodic with sidereality,

As ᵐᵘˡKAK.SI.DI (in Sumerian)
Saw through haphazard clay to innermost
Armatures of light whereby the ghost
Walks in a twinkling he has learned to scan.

*

Where has time flown? Since I began
You've learned to stand for seconds, balancing,
And look away at my approach, coyly.
My braincells continue to snuff out like sparks
At the average rate of 100,000 a day—
The intellect suspiciously resembling
Eddington's universe in headlong flight
From itself. A love I'd been taking nightly
Readings of sets behind the foliage now;
I wonder what will rise next from the sea—
The heart, no less suspiciously,
Remaining geocentric. Of an evening
I creak downstairs, unshaven in my robe,
Jaw with your father in his undershirt.
He's worn out by a day of spreading tar
Overtime upon America.
The TV off, you and your sister sleeping,
Your mother lifts from needlework a face
Lovelier, I find, without make-up,
Even as worry stitches her white brow:

She's written twice, and sent the photographs.
Silence from her people, weeks of it.
I've asked myself how much the godfather
They picked contributes to imbroglio.
Someone more orthodox . . .? I'll never know.
Who ever does? From the start, his fine frank grin,
Her fine nearsighted gaze said *Take us in.*
Let them make anything they liked of me
From personal effect to destiny.
Now should he reappraise or she regret,
Fly back, why don't they? We've a daily jet.
Ah but time lost, missed payments—they're in deep.
Listen. Your sister whimpering, her sleep
Dislocated, going on three years.
Some days the silver cloud is lined with tears.
(Another day, when letters thriftily
Stamped for surface mail arrive,
Connecticut is heaven once again.)
And what if I'd done nothing, where would *you* be?
"One more baby back there in the Greece,"
Your father firmly putting his best face
On pros and cons, "when every day make seven
Bucks at the foundry? Never in my life.
Why I say to mean, this kid, she yours!"
Let's hope that my expression reassures.

Finding a moment, I've written: *Rose from bed*
Where I'd begun imagining the baptism
(In my old faith bed was the baptism)
To dress for it. Then all of us were racing
The highway to a dozen finishing lines
Every last one unquotable, scored through,
You bubbling milk, your sister in my lap
Touching her rhinestone treble clef barrette
—Made-up touches. Lately I forget
The actual as it happens (Plato warns us
Writing undermines the memory—

So does photography, I should tell your father)
And have, as now, less memory than a mind
To rescue last month's Lethe-spattered module
From inner space—eternal black-on-white
Pencilings, moondusty palindrome—
For splashdown in the rainbow. Welcome home.

Let evening be at its height. Let me have stolen
Past the loud dance, its goat-eyed leader steadied
By the bull-shouldered next in line,
And found you being changed. Let your mother, proudly
Displaying under the nightie's many-eyeleted
Foam a marvelous "ripe olive" mole
Beside your navel, help me to conceive
That fixed, imaginary, starless pole
Of the ecliptic which this one we steer by
Circles, a notch each time the old bring golden
Gifts to the newborn child, whose age begins.
Nothing that cosmic in our case, my dear—
Just your parents' Iron Age yielding
To some twilight of the worldly goods.
Or myself dazed by dawnings as yet half sheer
Lyric convention, half genetic glow
("May she live for you!" guests call as they go)
Which too will pass. Meanwhile, à propos of ages,
Let this one of mine you usher in
Bending still above your crib enthralled,

Godchild, be lightly taken, life and limb,
By rosy-fingered flexings as by flame.
Who else would linger so, crooning your name,
But second childhood. When time came for him—

For me, that is—to go upstairs, one hitch
Was that our ups and downs meant so much more
Than the usual tralala from floor to floor.
Now I was seeing double—which was which?

Verse for Urania

No thing but stumbled toward its heavenly twin,
No thought but helped its subject to undress . . .
(Mother of that hour's muse, Forgetfulness,
Hold me strictly to the might-have-been.)

Each plate shattered below, each cry, each hue,
Any old composer could fix that
(Purcell? His "Blessed Virgin"? Strauss's "Bat"?)
Unless my taste had gone to pieces, too.

Well, light a lamp, but only long enough
To put the former on the turntable.
Head back, feet up, watch dark revolving fill
With coloratura, farthingale and ruff,

A schoolgirl's flight to Egypt, sore afraid,
Clasping the infant, thorn against her breast,
Through dotted quaver and too fleeting rest
The clavecin's dry fronds too thinly shade.

The text she sang was hackwork—Nahum Tate—
Yet ending: *Whilst of thy dear sight beguil'd,*
I trust the God, but O! I fear the Child.
Exactly my own feelings. It was late

And early. I had seen you through shut eyes.
Our bond was sacred, being secular:
In time embedded, it in us, near, far,
Flooding both levels with the same sunrise.

270

THE WILL

I am standing among the coal black
Walls of a living room that is
Somehow both David the Wise's and not his.
Outside, the dead of winter, wailing, bleak.

Two men and a woman, dressed in black,
Enter with a will. A will of mine?
They nod encouragement. I sign,
Give each my hand in parting. Now to pack

This canvas tote-bag. I have wrapped in jeans
With manuscript on either side for wadding
Something I'm carrying to a . . . to a wedding . . .

Then, wondering as always what it means
And what else I'm forgetting,
On my cold way. A car is waiting.

(Only last night a person more urbane
Than usual was heading for the Seine.

Here was one façade he seemed to know
From times he'd seen it all aglow

And heard its old chronologist pronounce
It not the present but the thought that counts.

He rang impulsively. No bell
Resounded from within the dark hotel.

Its front door, Roman-numeralled,
Still said "I" in white-on-emerald.

Some humbler way into the edifice
Was chalked just legibly "I*bis*."

The Will

Steam from a sudden manhole bore
Wetness to the dream. I woke heartsore.)

I'm at an airport, waiting. The scar itches.
Carving, last month I nearly removed my thumb.
Where was my mind? Lapses like this become
Standard practice. Not all of them leave me in stitches.

In growing puzzlement I've felt things losing
Their grip on me. What's done is done, dreamlike;
Clutches itself too late to stop the oozing
Reds, the numbing inward leak

Of pressures we have effortlessly risen
Through on occasion to a brilliant
Ice blue and white sestet

Six lines six miles above, if not rhyme, reason.
Its winged shadow tiny as an ant
Keeps up far down, state after sunnier state,

Or grown huge (have we landed?)
Scatters into human shadows all
Underfoot skittering through the terminal
To greet, lulled, blinded,

The mild, moist South. Che puro ciel . . .
I'm riding in a taxi. The lightskinned
Driver steering me through scenery skeined
With twitterings, flutterings, scrim of shell

Pink, shell ivory—O dogwood days—
Fleet against unutterably slow
Dynastic faces of a portico,

These float from view, lids quiver, the air dies
Upon my lips, the bag's bulk at my feet
Gone underwater-weightless, tempting fate.

My burden is an old wall-eyed stone-blond
Ibis. Over the years (I bought it with
A check my father wrote before his death)
I took to heart its funerary chic

Winged like a sandal, necked like the snakes on a wand,
Stalker that spears *and* spares . . .
Which passing into a young, happy pair's
Keeping could stand for the giver. Now, next week

I mean to remember to take
David the Fair's acrylics
And turn the wooden base to baked blue brick
With lotus frieze, blossom and pad and calyx,

Abstraction of a river, eau de Nil
Arrested by the powerful curving bill.

Gliding to a halt, the prodigal stirs.
Pays the driver. Gives himself up to home.
His mother, a year younger, kisses him.
Maids are wafting suitcases upstairs

While sirens over seventy, with names
Like Myra, Robin, Rosalie and Midge,
Call from the sun porch, "Come play bridge!"
They love their sweetly-sung bloodthirsty games.

He is sitting at the table, dealing,
When a first tentative wrong note
Is quickly taken up ("What is it, darling?")

The Will

By the whole orchestra in unison.
The unbid heart pounds in his throat—
The bag, the bird—left in the taxi—gone!

Gone for good. In the first shock of
Knowing it he tries
To play the dummy, dreads to advertise,
"Drinks water" like a character in Chekhov.

Life dims and parches. Self-inflicted
Desolation a faint horselaugh jars.
Property lies toppled, seeing stars
Nowhere in the dry dreambed reflected.

So that tonight's pint-size amphibian
Wriggler from murky impulse to ethereal act
Must hazard the dimensions of a man

Of means. Of meanings. Codicil
And heir alike. White-lipped survivor hacked
Out of his own will.

U DID WELL JM TO DISINHERIT
YR SELF & FRIENDS OF THAT STONE BIRD
—It's June, we're at the Ouija board,
David the True and I and our familiar spirit—

SACRED TO THOTH NOW AT 310 KNOX DRIVE
MACON GA IT HAS BROUGHT DISASTER
COMME TOUJOURS PARALYZED THE DRIVERS SISTER
MAXINE SHAW BORN 1965

THESE BALEFUL PRESENCES SHAPED FOR THE DEAD
WHEN THEY CHANGE HANDS EXACT A SACRIFICE
REMEMBER ITS FIRST YEAR CHEZ VOUS YR FACE
TURNED VOTIVE GOLD JAUNDICE THE DOCTOR SD

274

GODS BEAK SAY I EMBEDDED IN YR SIDE
HARDLY THE BIBELOT TO GIVE A BRIDE

Ephraim, we take you with a grain of salt,
Protagonist at best of the long story
Sketches and notes for which were my missing bag's
Other significant cargo, by the way.

BY THE WAY SINCE U DID NOT CONSULT
THEIR SUBJECT YR GLUM PAGES LACKED HIS GLORY
That stings. The guide and I lock horns like stags.
What is *his* taste? Aquinas? Bossuet?

SOIS SAGE DEAR HEART & SET MY TEACHINGS DOWN
Why, Ephraim, you belong to the old school—
You think the Word by definition good.

IF U DO NOT YR WORLD WILL BE UNDONE
& HEAVEN ITSELF TURN TO ONE GRINNING SKULL
So? We must write to save the face of God?

With which the teacup pointer goes inert.
Ephraim, are you still there? Angry? Hurt?

Long pause. YR SPIRIT HAS BEEN CAUGHT REDHANDED
IT IS HIS OCCUPATIONAL FAIBLESSE
TO ENTER & POSSESS REPEAT POSSESS
L OBJET AIME   Who, me? WELL I HAD PLANNED IT

WITHOUT SO MANY DAVIDS TO COMBAT
MY GIANT DESIGNS UPON YR ART MON CHER
SHRINK TO THIS TOPSYTURVY WILLOWWARE
IGLOO WALTZING WITH THE ALPHABET

The Will

So what is the next step? LIVE MORE LIVE MOST
EXPECTING NO RETURN   To earth?   IT SEEMS
U WILL NOT   Hush, don't tell us— PLEASANT DREAMS
GIVE UP EVERYTHING EXCEPT THE GHOST

I'm at my desk. Paralysis.
No headway through the drafts
Before me—bleaching wastes and drifts
Of time spent writing (or not writing) this.

Then a lucky stroke unearths the weird
Basalt passage of last winter,
Tunneling black. The match struck as I enter
Illuminates . . . My word!

(At someone's bidding smooth white plaster
Had been incised with mourning slave and master

And pets with mystic attributes
In profile among goblets, fans and fruits.

Here was a manuscript. Here were
Five catgut stitches laid in lusterware.

And here in final state, where lost was found,
The ibis sat. Another underground

Chamber made ready. If this one was not
Quite the profoundest or the most ornate,

Give it time. The bric-a-brac
Slumbered in bonds that of themselves would break

One fine day, at any chance unsealing,
To shining leaf and woken shades of feeling.)

Already thickskinned little suns
Are coming back, and gusts of sharp cologne
—Lemon trees bearing and in bloom at once—

And rings exchanged for life,
And one high jet that cut to the blue's bone
Its healing hieroglyph,

While briefly over the house
A dirtbrown helicopter
Like the bad fairy Carabosse, its clatter
Drowning out the vows,

Drowning out the sweet
Voices of doves and finches
At home among the branches
In the bright, cool heat,

Hovered close, then, seeing
That it would not eclipse
The sunniness beneath it, up and went

As much had, without saying—
Leaving to lovers' lips
All further argument.

LOST IN TRANSLATION

for Richard Howard

Diese Tage, die leer dir scheinen
und wertlos für das All,
haben Wurzeln zwischen den Steinen
und trinken dort überall.

A card table in the library stands ready
To receive the puzzle which keeps never coming.
Daylight shines in or lamplight down
Upon the tense oasis of green felt.
Full of unfulfillment, life goes on,
Mirage arisen from time's trickling sands
Or fallen piecemeal into place:
German lesson, picnic, see-saw, walk
With the collie who "did everything but talk"—
Sour windfalls of the orchard back of us.
A summer without parents is the puzzle,
Or should be. But the boy, day after day,
Writes in his Line-a-Day *No puzzle.*

He's in love, at least. His French Mademoiselle,
In real life a widow since Verdun,
Is stout, plain, carrot-haired, devout.
She prays for him, as does a curé in Alsace,
Sews costumes for his marionettes,
Helps him to keep behind the scene
Whose sidelit goosegirl, speaking with his voice,
Plays Guinevere as well as Gunmoll Jean.
Or else at bedtime in his tight embrace
Tells him her own French hopes, her German fears,
Her—but what more is there to tell?
Having known grief and hardship, Mademoiselle
Knows little more. Her languages. Her place.

Noon coffee. Mail. The watch that also waited
Pinned to her heart, poor gold, throws up its hands—
No puzzle! Steaming bitterness
Her sugars draw pops back into his mouth, translated:
"Patience, chéri. Geduld, mein Schatz."
(Thus, reading Valéry the other evening
And seeming to recall a Rilke version of "Palme,"
That sunlit paradigm whereby the tree
Taps a sweet wellspring of authority,
The hour came back. Patience dans l'azur.
Geduld im . . . Himmelblau? Mademoiselle.)

Out of the blue, as promised, of a New York
Puzzle-rental shop the puzzle comes—
A superior one, containing a thousand hand-sawn,
Sandal-scented pieces. Many take
Shapes known already—the craftsman's repertoire
Nice in its limitation—from other puzzles:
Witch on broomstick, ostrich, hourglass,
Even (surely not just in retrospect)
An inchling, innocently branching palm.
These can be put aside, made stories of
While Mademoiselle spreads out the rest face-up,
Herself excited as a child; or questioned
Like incoherent faces in a crowd,
Each with its scrap of highly colored
Evidence the Law must piece together.
Sky-blue ostrich? Likely story.
Mauve of the witch's cloak white, severed fingers
Pluck? Detain her. The plot thickens
As all at once two pieces interlock.

Mademoiselle does borders—(Not so fast.
A London dusk, December last.
Chatter silenced in the library
This grown man reenters, wearing grey.
A medium. All except him have seen

Panel slid back, recess explored,
An object at once unique and common
Displayed, planted in a plain tole
Casket the subject now considers
Through shut eyes, saying in effect:
"Even as voices reach me vaguely
A dry saw-shriek drowns them out,
Some loud machinery—a lumber mill?
Far uphill in the fir forest
Trees tower, tense with shock,
Groaning and cracking as they crash groundward.
But hidden here is a freak fragment
Of a pattern complex in appearance only.
What it seems to show is superficial
Next to that long-term lamination
Of hazard and craft, the karma that has
Made it matter in the first place.
Plywood, Piece of a puzzle." Applause
Acknowledged by an opening of lids
Upon the thing itself. A sudden dread—
But to go back. All this lay years ahead.)

Mademoiselle does borders. Straight-edge pieces
Align themselves with earth or sky
In twos and threes, naive cosmogonists
Whose views clash. Nomad inlanders meanwhile
Begin to cluster where the totem
Of a certain vibrant egg-yolk yellow
Or pelt of what emerging animal
Acts on the straggler like a trumpet call
To form a more sophisticated unit.
By suppertime two ragged wooden clouds
Have formed. In one, a Sheik with beard
And flashing sword hilt (he is all but finished)
Steps forward on a tiger skin. A piece
Snaps shut, and fangs gnash out at us!
In the second cloud—they gaze from cloud to cloud
With marked if undecipherable feeling—

Most of a dark-eyed woman veiled in mauve
Is being helped down from her camel (kneeling)
By a small backward-looking slave or page-boy
(Her son, thinks Mademoiselle mistakenly)
Whose feet have not been found. But lucky finds
In the last minutes before bed
Anchor both factions to the scene's limits
And, by so doing, orient
Them eye to eye across the green abyss.
The yellow promises, oh bliss,
To be in time a sumptuous tent.

Puzzle begun I write in the day's space,
Then, while she bathes, peek at Mademoiselle's
Page to the curé: ". . . cette innocente mère,
Ce pauvre enfant, que deviendront-ils?"
Her azure script is curlicued like pieces
Of the puzzle she will be telling him about.
(Fearful incuriosity of childhood!
"Tu as l'accent allemand," said Dominique.
Indeed. Mademoiselle was only French by marriage.
Child of an English mother, a remote
Descendant of the great explorer Speke,
And Prussian father. No one knew. I heard it
Long afterwards from her nephew, a UN
Interpreter. His matter-of-fact account
Touched old strings. My poor Mademoiselle,
With 1939 about to shake
This world where "each was the enemy, each the friend"
To its foundations, kept, though signed in blood,
Her peace a shameful secret to the end.)
"Schlaf wohl, chéri." Her kiss. Her thumb
Crossing my brow against the dreams to come.

This World that shifts like sand, its unforeseen
Consolations and elate routine,
Whose Potentate had lacked a retinue?
Lo! it assembles on the shrinking Green.

Gunmetal-skinned or pale, all plumes and scars,
Of Vassalage the noblest avatars—
The very coffee-bearer in his vair
Vest is a swart Highness, next to ours.

Kef easing Boredom, and iced syrups, thirst,
In guessed-at glooms old wives who know the worst
Outsweat that virile fiction of the New:
"Insh'Allah, he will tire—" "—or kill her first!"

(Hardly a proper subject for the Home,
Work of—dear Richard, I shall let *you* comb
Archives and learned journals for his name—
A minor lion attending on Gérôme.)

While, thick as Thebes whose presently complete
Gates close behind them, Houri and Afreet
Both claim the Page. He wonders whom to serve,
And what his duties are, and where his feet,

And if we'll find, as some before us did,
That piece of Distance deep in which lies hid
Your tiny apex sugary with sun,
Eternal Triangle, Great Pyramid!

Then Sky alone is left, a hundred blue
Fragments in revolution, with no clue
To where a Niche will open. Quite a task,
Putting together Heaven, yet we do.

It's done. Here under the table all along
Were those missing feet. It's done.

The dog's tail thumping. Mademoiselle sketching
Costumes for a coming harem drama
To star the goosegirl. All too soon the swift
Dismantling. Lifted by two corners,

The puzzle hung together—and did not.
Irresistibly a populace
Unstitched of its attachments, rattled down.
Power went to pieces as the witch
Slithered easily from Virtue's gown.
The blue held out for time, but crumbled, too.
The city had long fallen, and the tent,
A separating sauce mousseline,
Been swept away. Remained the green
On which the grown-ups gambled. A green dusk.
First lightning bugs. Last glow of west
Green in the false eyes of (coincidence)
Our mangy tiger safe on his bared hearth.

Before the puzzle was boxed and readdressed
To the puzzle shop in the mid-Sixties,
Something tells me that one piece contrived
To stay in the boy's pocket. How do I know?
I know because so many later puzzles
Had missing pieces—Maggie Teyte's high notes
Gone at the war's end, end of the vogue for collies,
A house torn down; and hadn't Mademoiselle
Kept back her pitiful bit of truth as well?
I've spent the last days, furthermore,
Ransacking Athens for that translation of "Palme."
Neither the Goethchaus nor the National Library
Seems able to unearth it. Yet I can't
Just be imagining. I've seen it. Know
How much of the sun-ripe original
Felicity Rilke made himself forego
(Who loved French words—verger, mûr, parfumer)
In order to render its underlying sense.
Know already in that tongue of his
What Pains, what monolithic Truths
Shadow stanza to stanza's symmetrical
Rhyme-rutted pavement. Know that ground plan left
Sublime and barren, where the warm Romance
Stone by stone faded, cooled; the fluted nouns

283

Made taller, lonelier than life
By leaf-carved capitals in the afterglow.
The owlet umlaut peeps and hoots
Above the open vowel. And after rain
A deep reverberation fills with stars.

Lost, is it, buried? One more missing piece?

But nothing's lost. Or else: all is translation
And every bit of us is lost in it
(Or found—I wander through the ruin of S
Now and then, wondering at the peacefulness)
And in that loss a self-effacing tree,
Color of context, imperceptibly
Rustling with its angel, turns the waste
To shade and fiber, milk and memory.

From Late Settings (1985)

GRASS

The river irises
Draw themselves in.
Enough to have seen
Their day. The arras

Also of evening drawn,
We light up between
Earth and Venus
On the courthouse lawn,

Kept by this cheerful
Inch of green
And ten more years—fifteen?—
From disappearing.

CLEARING THE TITLE

for DJ

Because the wind has changed, because I guess
My poem (what to call it though?) is finished,
Because the golden genie chafes within
His smudged-glass bottle and, god help us, you
Have chosen, sight unseen, this tropic rendezvous
Where tourist, outcast and in-groupie gather
Island by island, linked together,
Causeways bridging the vast shallowness—

Through the low ceiling motors rip.
Below me, twisting in the asphalt grip
Of mall and pancake house, boatel and bank,
What's left of Nature here? Those trees five thousand tin
Roofs, like little mirrors in distress,
Would flash up from if the sun were out . . .
Oh for the lucid icebound book of winter
I gave up my rapt place in for this trip!

Such a mistake—past fifty and behaving
As if hope sprang eternal. At the baggage claim
Armed with "The Power and the Glory" (Greene),
I notice, finger-drawn in a soaped pane,
One black sun only, spokes in air
Like feelers of a bug flipped on its back,
Above a clumsy WELLCOME TO THE KEYS
—Then see the open car. You in it, waving.

Couldn't one have gone into the matter
Before succumbing? Easier said than done,
What with this tough white coral skeleton
Beneath a crop of shanties built on blocks,
On air, on edge for, any day,
Water and wind to sweep them clean away.
Meanwhile I'm braced, capricious chatterbox,
Against your blasts of horn and flood of casual patter.

Sales patter? The appalling truth now bores
Into my brain: you've *bought* a house
And pass, en route to it, the peeling white
Five-story skyscraper in which "our" title
Is being cleared!—activity no more
Thinkable (you park, fling a green-painted door
Open onto a fresh white hall)
Than what the termites do, look! to these floors

Between the muddy varnish of whose lines
(But can you picture *living* here? Expect
Me to swelter, year by sunset year,
Beneath these ceilings?—which at least aren't low.
What about houses elsewhere, rooms already packed
With memories? That chiffonier
Would have to go, or else be painted white . . .)
More brightly with each word the daylight shines.

And fresh as paint the bare rooms, if you please,
Having consumed whatever came before,
Look up unblinking: will *we* bring
Their next meal—table, mirror, bed, lamp, chair?
Serve the ravenous interior
With real-life victuals, voices, vanities
Until it lolls back purring?—like our slum
Garden zonked by milk-bombs from two old bent trees.

Presuming, then, tripod and pendulum
Tell truly, and the freckled county clerk
Completes, adds to the master file
A Gothic-lettered "title" with your name—
What happens next? Behind a latticework
Of deeds no one has time or patience to undo
We cultivate our little lot, meanwhile
Waiting companionably for kingdom come?

Clearing the Title

Close-ups: hibiscus broad as garden hats.
Large winged but nameless insect excavated
By slaves; the abdomen's deep strata
Primitive-intricate, like macramé.
Then from beneath the house, fee fi fo fum!
Caller the color of good smoke blown through the years
Into this dumb scarred mug he lifts to say:
"Huh? Not want *me*? Man, the whole world wants *cats*!"

No. No, no, no. We can't just cast
Three decades' friendships and possessions out.
Who're our friends here? (In fact I recognize
Old ones everywhere I turn my eyes—
Trumpet-vine, cracked pavement, that faint sulphur smell,
Those see-through lizards, quick as a heartbeat . . .)
But people? (Well, the Wilburs live downstreet . . .)
Of course, if shutting doors onto the past

Could damage *it* . . . Wherever that thought led,
Turning the loose knob onto better-late-
Than-never light, we breast its deepening stream
Along with others who've a date
With sunset. Each day's unspent zinc or red brass penny
—Here at land's end not deposited
In winter palisades crowned by antennae,
Fuel for the all-night talk shows of the dead—

Inflates to moidore, melts toward an oblivion
Alone, its gravity unspecified,
The far-off mangrove islet saves
From being wholly formed of air and waves,
Of light and birdcry, as with each step less
Divides the passer-through from, what to call
Such radiance—creative? terminal?
Day's flush of pleasure, knowing its poem done?

Our poem now. It's signed JM, but grew
From life together, grain by coral grain.
Building on it, we let the life cloud over . . .
Time to break through those clouds, for heaven's sake,
And look round. Any place will do
(Remember, later at the discothèque)
And what at first appall precisely are the changes
That everybody is entitled to.

Here at the end's a landing stage swept clean
Of surplus "properties" and "characters".
Gone the thick banyan, the opaque old queen.
Only some flimsiest human veil
Woven of trickster and revivalist,
Musician and snake-charmer (and, yes, us as well)
Pot- and patchouli-scented floats between
The immense warm pink spotlight and the scene.

Here's the Iguana Man, from lands
"Beneath the world". Dragons, withered like him,
Unwinking drape his fishnet singlet. Here
Balloons are straining for release; we pick
A headstrong silver one. And here a clown
Cat-limber, white-lipped with a bright cerulean tear
On one rouged cheek, rides unicycle, hands
Nonchalantly juggling firebrands.

Circles round every act form, or to groans
Disperse. This portion of the dock's been cleared
By the Salvation Army. (They're
Nine strong, a family; beneath the same
Grim visor glowers, babe to grandmother,
The same grim love.) "Y'all give!" our deadpan clown
Yells brandishing a hammer fit for Thor,
"Give or Ah'll clobber yew!" and *grunt* go the trombones.

Though no one does, no thunder strikes. Because—
Say, because a black girl with shaved skull
Sways on the brink: flexed knee and ankle-bell
And eyes that burn back at the fiery ball
Till it relenting tests with one big toe
Its bath, and Archimedean splendors overflow.
As the sun sets, "Let's hear it for the sun!"
Cry voices. Laughter. Bells. Applause

(Think of the dead here, sleeping above ground
—Simpler than to hack a tomb from coral—
In whitewashed hope chests under the palm fronds.
Or think of waking, whether to the quarrel
Of white cat and black crow, those unchanged friends,
Or to a dazzle from below:
Earth visible through floor-cracks, miles—or inches—down,
And spun by a gold key-chain round and round . . .)

Whereupon on high, where all is bright
Day still, blue turning to key lime, to steel
A clear flame-dusted crimson bars,
Sky puts on the face of the young clown
As the balloons, mere hueless dots now, stars
Or periods—although tonight we trust no real
Conclusions will be reached—float higher yet,
Juggled slowly by the changing light.

ISLAND IN THE WORKS

From air seen fathom-deep
But rising to a head—
Abscess of the abyss
Any old night letting rip
Its fires, yearlong,
As roundabout waves hiss—

Jaded by untold blue
Subversions, watered-down
Moray and Spaniard . . .
Now to construe
In the original
Those at first arid, hard,

Soon rootfast, ramifying,
Always more fruitful
Dialogues with light.
Various dimwit under-
graduate types will wonder
At my calm height,

Vapors by then surmounted
(Merely another phase?)
And how in time I trick
Out my new "shores" and "bays"
With small craft, shrimpers'
Bars and rhetoric.

Darkly the Old Ones grumble
I'll hate all that. Hate words,
Their schooling flame?
The spice grove chatted up
By small gray knowing birds?
Myself given a name?

Island in the Works

Waves, as your besetting
Depth-wish recedes,
I'm surfacing, I'm home!
Open the atlas. Here:
This dot, securely netted
Under the starry dome.

(Unlike this page—no sooner
Brought to the pool than wafted
Out of reach, laid flat
Face-up on cool glares, ever
So lightly swayed, or swaying . . .
Now who did that?)

THINK TANK

Because our young were drab
And slow to grow, for Carnival we ate them,
Pennants of motley distancing the deed
In the dechlorinated crystal slab.

The harlequin all grace and greed
Made glancing mincemeat of the mirror kissed.
The scholar blotched with ich
Sank into lonely shudderings.

But at our best we were of one mind,
Did our own sick or vital things
Within a medium secured by trick

Reflections over which, day, night, the braille
Eraser glided of the Snail
Our servant, huge and blind.

THE PIER: UNDER PISCES

The shallows, brighter,
Wetter than water,
Tepidly glitter with the fingerprint-
Obliterating feel of kerosene.

Each piling like a totem
Rises from rock bottom
Straight through the ceiling
Aswirl with suns, clear ones or pale bluegreen,

And beyond! where bubbles burst,
Sphere of their worst dreams,
If dream is what they do,
These floozy fish—

Ceramic-lipped in filmy
Peekaboo blouses,
Fluorescent body
Stockings, hot stripes,

Swayed by the hypnotic ebb and flow
Of supermarket Muzak,
Bolero beat the undertow's
Pebble-filled gourds repeat;

Jailbait consumers of subliminal
Hints dropped from on high
In gobbets none
Eschews as minced kin;

Who, hooked themselves—bamboo diviner
Bent their way
Vigorously nodding
Encouragement—

Are one by one hauled kisswise, oh
Into some blinding hell
Policed by leathery ex-
Justices each

Minding his catch, if catch is what he can,
If mind is what one means—
The torn mouth
Stifled by newsprint, working still. If . . . if . . .

The little scales
Grow stiff. Dusk plugs her dryer in,
Buffs her nails, riffles through magazines,
While far and wide and deep

Rove the great sharkskin-suited criminals
And safe in this lit shrine
A boy sits. He'll be eight.
We've drunk our milk, we've eaten our stringbeans,

But left untasted on the plate
The fish. An eye, a broiled pearl, meeting mine,
I lift his fork . . .
The bite. The tug of fate.

DOMINO

Delicious, white, refined
Is all that I was raised to be,
Whom feeling for the word
Plus crystal rudiments of mind
Still keep—however stirred—
From wholly melting in the tea.

Far, far away, men cut
The sea-wide, sea-green fields of cane.
Often a child's lament
Filled the infested hut.
Doña Pilar flew back for Lent
—Had she been inhumane?

The better to appraise his mess,
History's health freak begs
That such as we be given up.
Outpouring bitterness
Rewards the drainer of the cup . . .
He'll miss those sparkling dregs.

THE SCHOOL PLAY

"Harry of Hereford, Lancaster, and Derby,
Stands here for God, his country, and . . ." And what?
"Stands here for God, his Sovereign, and himself,"
Growled Captain Fry who had the play by heart.
I was the First Herald, "a small part"
—I was small too—"but an important one."
What was not important to the self
At nine or ten? Already I had crushes
On Mowbray, Bushy, and the Duke of York.
Handsome Donald Niemann (now himself,
According to the Bulletin, headmaster
Of his own school somewhere out West) awoke
Too many self-indulgent mouthings in
The dummy mirror before smashing it,
For me to set my scuffed school cap at him.
Another year I'd play that part myself,
Or Puck, or Goneril, or Prospero.
Later, in adolescence, it was thought
Clever to speak of having found oneself,
With a smile and rueful headshake for those who hadn't.
People still do. Only the other day
A woman my age told us that her son
"Hadn't found himself"—at thirty-one!
I heard in the mind's ear an amused hum
Of mothers and fathers from beyond the curtain,
And that flushed, far-reaching hour came back
Months of rehearsal in the gymnasium
Had led to: when the skinny nobodies
Who'd memorized the verse and learned to speak it
Emerged in beards and hose (or gowns and rouge)
Vivid with character, having put themselves
All unsuspecting into the masters' hands.

DAYS OF 1941 AND '44

for David Mixsell

The nightmare shower room. My tormentor leers
In mock lust—surely?—at my crotch.
The towel I reach for held just out of reach,
I gaze back petrified, past speech, past tears.

Or Saturday night war games. Shy of the whole
Student body, and my own, I've hid
In the furnace room. His warning stokes my head:
This time, Toots, it's your pants up the flagpole!

And why, four-letter man, descend
To pick on me, in those days less than nothing,
A shaky X on panic's bottom line?

Imagine meeting now, here at the end—
You sheep-eyed, stripped of your wolf's clothing—
And seeing which came true, your life or mine.

At Silver Springs, that Easter break,
I'd noted "heavenly colors and swell fish"
—Mismarriage of maternal gush
To regular-guy. By evening: "Bellyache."

I was *fifteen*? Dear god. Page after page,
Fury and rapture, smudge and curlicue,
One ugly duckling waddled through
The awkward age.

A month of sundaes, gym excuses, play
("I got the part!!") and "long walk with S. J."
Locate the diarist away at school

Right after the divorce. Would brat-
tishness that ripe for ridicule
Ever be resorbed like baby fat?

300

"A lord of Life, a prince of Prose"—
Alliterations courtesy of Wilde.
Another year, with such as these to wield,
I won the Fourth Form Essay Prize.

In vain old Mr Raymond's sky-blue stare
Paled with revulsion when I spoke to him
About my final paper. "Jim,"
He quavered, "don't, *don't* write on Baudelaire."

But viewed from deep in my initial
Aesthetic phase, brought like a lukewarm bath to
Fizzy life by those mauve salts,

Paradises (and if artificial
So much the better) promised more than Matthew
Arnold. Faith rose dripping from the false.

My dear—yes, let that stand: you were my first
True hate. You whispering, the sadist's glee.
You lounging, buried in my diary—
Each phrase a fuse. I wanted you to burst.

Your cubicle across from mine was bleak
As when school opened. Oh, *you* didn't need
Cushions, posters, cotton for nosebleed,
A mother caught by flash in Red Cross chic.

Or did you? Three more years and you would die,
For lack of them perhaps, in France, at war.
Word reached me one hot twilight. It was raining,

Clay spattering the barracks. I
Fell back onto my bunk, parched for decor,
With *Swann's Way*. Basic training . . .

I'd have my France at war's end. Over highballs
Back home, would show that certain of us *were* up
To the museums and cafés of Europe—
Those peeling labels!

Rich boy you called me. True, there'd be no turning
Back from the mixed blessings of a first-rate
Education exquisitely offset
By an inbred contempt for learning.

And true, when money traveled, talent stayed
Deep in the trunk, assuming it got packed.
Mine was a harmless figment? If you like.

Remember, though, how untrained eyes subtract
From the coin-glint of a summer glade
The adder coiled to strike.

The nothing you'd become took on a weight
No style I knew could lighten. The latrine
Mirrors that night observed what once had been
Your mortal enemy disintegrate

To multiabsent and bone-tired hoplite,
Tamed more than told apart by his dog-tags.
Up the flagpole with those rank fatigues
Bunched round his boots! Another night

Beneath unsimulated fire he'd crawl
With full pack, rifle, helmeted, weak-kneed,
And peeking upward see the tracers scrawl

Their letter of atonement, then the flare
Quote its entire red minefield from midair—
Between whose lines it has been life to read.

PAGE FROM THE KORAN

A small vellum environment
Overrun by black
Scorpions of Kufic script—their ranks
All trigger tail and gold vowel-sac—
At auction this mild winter morning went
For six hundred Swiss francs.

By noon, fire from the same blue heavens
Had half erased Beirut.
Allah be praised, it said on crude handbills,
For guns and Nazarenes to shoot.
"How gladly with proper words," said Wallace Stevens,
"The soldier dies." Or kills.

God's very word, then, stung the heart
To greed and rancor. Yet
Not where the last glow touches one spare man
Inked-in against his minaret
—Letters so handled they are life, and hurt,
Leaving the scribe immune?

TOPICS

1. CASUAL WEAR

Your average tourist: Fifty. 2.3
Times married. Dressed, this year, in Ferdi Plinthbower
Originals. Odds 1 to 9^{10}
Against her strolling past the Embassy

Today at noon. Your average terrorist:
Twenty-five. Celibate. No use for trends,
At least in clothing. Mark, though, where it ends.
People have come forth made of colored mist

Unsmiling on one hundred million screens
To tell of his prompt phone call to the station,
"Claiming responsibility"—devastation
Signed with a flourish, like the dead wife's jeans.

2. POPULAR DEMAND

These few deep strongholds. Each with generator,
Provisions, dossiers. It would seem the worst
Has happened, who knows how—essential data
Lost in the bright, chromosome-garbling burst.

You, Comrade, will indefinitely be resident
Of this one, with your disciplined women and staff;
You and yours of this one, Mr. President.
Grim huddles. Then a first, uncertain laugh

—Spirits reviving, as life's bound to do?
Not from dead land, waste water, sulphur sky.
Nowhere is anything both alive and blue
Except, inside your block heads, the mind's eye

304

Marveling up out of our common grave:
You never thought . . . Sincerely didn't think . . .
Who gave it clearance? It ransacks the cave
For you with cordial venom. Damn you, drink!

3. CAESARION

A glow of cells in the warm Sea,
Some vaguest green or violet soup
Took a few billion days to loop
The loops we called Eternity.

Before the splendor bit its tail
Blake rendered it in aquatint
And Eddington pursued a glint—
Recoil, explosion—scale on scale.

What stellar hopefuls, plumed like Mars,
Sank to provincial rant and strut,
Lines blown, within the occiput?
Considering the fate of stars,

I think that man died happiest
Who never saw his Mother clasp
Fusion, the tiny naked asp,
By force of habit to her breast.

THE HOUSE FLY

Come October, if I close my eyes,
A self till then subliminal takes flight
Buzzing round me, settling upon the knuckle,
The lip to be explored not as in June
But with a sense verging on micromania
Of wrong, of tiny, hazy, crying wrongs
Which quite undo her—look at that zigzag totter,
Proboscis blindly tapping like a cane.
Gone? If so, only to re-alight

Or else in a stray beam resume the grand toilette
(Eggs of next year's mischief long since laid):
Unwearying strigils taken to the frayed,
Still glinting wings; the dull-red lacquer head
Lifted from its socket, turned mechanically
This way and that, like a wristwatch being wound,
As if there would always be time . . .

Downstairs in this same house one summer night,
Founding the cult, her ancestress alit
On the bare chest of Strato Mouflouzélis
Who stirred in the lamp-glow but did not wake.
To say so brings it back on every autumn
Feebler wings, and further from that Sun,
That mist-white wafer she and I partake of
Alone this afternoon, making a rite
Distinct from both the blessing and the blight.

SANTO

for Peter Hooten and Alan Moss Reverón

Francisco on his shelf,
Wreathed in dusty wax
Roses, for weeks and weeks
Hadn't been himself—

Making no day come true
By answering a prayer,
Just dully standing there . . .
What did our Grandma do?

She painted his beard black
And rinsed the roses clean,
Then hid his rags in half
A new red satin cloak,

Renaming him Martín.
Next week the baby spoke,
Juan sent a photograph
On board his submarine,

Aunt Concha went to cook
Downtown at the hotel,
The sick white dog got well
—And that was all it took!

PETER

Right arm: a many-splendored
Korean dagger-and-heart
Wound in a scroll, or banner—
DEATH BEFORE DISHONOR.

(Between the H and O
One barely audible
Stammer of skin,
DISH ONOR—SO.)

Then left: italic *Lillia,* herself
Far out in Venice West
With the car and the children, sinking
Painlessly in

Under a BB shot
Probed to this white star
Through deepening north woods where "Spring was best"
And "never human foot . . ."

But your chest, a boy's no longer,
Paler, leaner
From night shifts at the Mill:
Across it still, over your real heart—rainbow

Fixes of plumage all that while postponed—
The USA's storm-blue
Project of an eagle
Glides, with nothing in its claws but you.

2. BAD TRIP

Gray light. A cautious tread.
Your weight
On the bedside, shuddering—
Eighty million comets in your head!

Walking all night
Beach after beach, surfstrafe,
Starknout, clockwise flailings of the dark . . .
I want to think we're safe,

Each of us, in each day's golden scales.
From your unwinking stare
A juice of pain
Trickles between knuckles. There,

The tranquilizer's working. There, lie back,
Hush. Tears
Wetting the pillow touch
Its featherbrain

And soon enough a suite for solo pharynx
Clumsily bowed and scraped will find me bent,
A room away, on putting words
Into an angel's mouth. Thirty-eight years

No less the waif
Afraid of dark? Sunshine
Spread over hurt feet, snore to your heart's content
And mine.

Peter

3. FUTURE APPLES INC.

You've fallen on work.
Luck smiles her little smile, by legerdemain
Those knuckles turn to outcrop,
Those tricklings to a wind-creased pool,

And here's your form
Reflected in a farm!—
Gaunt, lightly, chronically stoned
Latterday Eden with its absentee

Landlord, its wary creatures. The mud-caked brush-hog
Loves no man yet, neither (to judge by scratches
On wrists and calves)
Do the blackberry patches.

Some trees then, old as wives,
But bearing. And uphill, a beard
Of second growth, fruitless perplexities,
Dead roots, bygone

Entanglements *away* from light
Beg to be cleared.
It's winter wheat, clover and timothy,
Seasons of sweetening

If young limbs are to climb
Where a brow's furrowed, and the first-born so deftly
Hefts his bushel that you blink astonished
From time to time.

4. THE FIRST-BORN

—Of *this* union.
Fact is, you've children everywhere,
Vermont, Korea, some
Grown-up enough to have kids of their own,

For misspelt pleas to come—
Illness, abortion, welfare and parole.
They all need help.
You're sorry and would like to help

But figure you help them more in the long run
By not helping now.
And so you grin and shrug
As at the mention of vasectomy—

Genetic litterbug!
This latest batch is "different"—still unscarred
By life, you mean?
In drifts the six-year-old

Wearing his mother's blouse (where's she?
Oh, "off on a rampage"),
Red polish on the fingernails
Of one hand. Drawn to me,

He lolls between my knees, asks *why* and *why*,
But listens also, much as if the die
Hadn't been cast. Will he have you—will I—
When all else fails?

Peter

5. "FIDELIO" FROM THE MET

Upon a certain rock
—Glacial warden over "dreams come true"—
You kept on building castles, no,
Dungeons in air,

Unspeakable, unvisitable glooms
Whose guiltless prisoner,
Wasted beyond recognition, was alive
Just barely, just because you were.

(How often in the city
I'd see you—boots, jeans, glasses, hair—
And shout. As if you could do better than
To look like everyman.)

Yet when that boulder you'd go sit on,
Peter, come night,
To smoke and watch the constellations
For its dislodging needed dynamite

And like the heaviest heart at freedom's trumpet
Leapt awkwardly an inch, and broke,
There was no question whose
Whole life, starwise along its faults, had started

To set the musical
Crystals, feldspar and quartz,
Aglow down pristine faces only now
Seeing the light.

LAST MORNINGS IN CALIFORNIA

Another misty one. These opaline
Emulsions of world and self. Paulette high up
In eucalyptus uttering her sun cry.
Arms reaching for the glimmer coming, going.

Tan shingle house, its hearth out cold, its tenant
Likewise, under patchwork. Fortune told
In Cups, a child on whom the Sun sweats fire,
The cards inverted, strewn, and his wild words

"Fool that one was and Hermit one now is,
Simple Death we'll both feel like tomorrow—"
Screwdrivers flecking the carpet with damp rust.
Of late a Guest, a further figure

Almost himself thanks to some B Complex
Taken in time, sits in the ferny alcove
Leafing a book of words Paulette appears to have learned
Never, never again to climb trees with.

She turns magnificent sane eyes upon this other's
Apparition. Strokes its grizzled beard
With gray-gloved fingers. Nearly gets to share
Its Danish when—a rent in air, the day's first

Thudding shudder (little hornet jet
Lonesome for Asia) sends the lemur flying
Into her master's limbs. His features dim and brighten
Working their way through night school. Every morning

The rip widens. At its edge a sun
Great white cloths equip will be wiping grime
From the tinted blue plate glass of fifty stories.
Perilous task. You wouldn't dare look down

On meditation center or shopping plaza.
One hard glance at the fault so many out here built on
And who knows? by noon another scarp upcoast,
Gilt broom and giant antennae, could be toppling

Dream material into some profounder
Pacific state—sea-boom, its thunder stolen
By the sleepers' softly breathing cave. Carnation
Pink to bone-white snippet stitched,

Laved past bleeding. Just one head, one tail
Protruding. Loud gin stilled and dyer's blues broadcast
On the spent wavelengths of the quilting bee . . .
Instead, the reader looks up "eucalyptus"

(From the Greek, *well-hidden*). Or if the sun has slipped
This once from its mile-high, breakneck ledge
To land somehow unhurt, all smiles,
Square in the suitcase he is living out of,

Goes—the cards have had him coming and going—
And kneels before the radiant disarray,
Clothing for days to come. On any one of them
Shutting the lid in a twinkling he'll be gone.

BRONZE

In August 1972 a skin-diver off Riace, on the Cala-brian coast, saw at a depth of seven or eight meters an arm upthrust from the sandy bottom. Having made sure that it was not of flesh, and remarking nearby a second, sanded-over form, he notified the local Archeological Museum. Frogmen easily raised the two figures. Even encrusted with silica and lime, they were from the start felt to be Greek originals. Their restoration, in Florence, would take nine years.

I

Birdsong. May. Tuscany. A house. Sunset
Through red or green panes falling on small print
Pored over by two figures: my companion
("David the Fair") still, after all these years,
Marvelously young, gentle in manner—yet
A certain eager bloom is lost, like wax,
To earn a new, inexorable glint;
Umberto then, our host, gnarled round his cane,
Long freckled hands refolding the timetable
Dense as himself with station and connection.
Triumphant stumps of silver light
His austere satyr's face. The morning train
To Florence will allow us, he opines,
Forty minutes with them, "all one needs.
The next train down will have you back for lunch."

Perfection—they won't be in such easy reach
Ever again. But guess who hesitates!
"Close connections," says too quiet a voice,
"Harm the soul." I stare (indeed,
So he has always thought) and check a groan.
He's been unwell—one must remember that;
Has no resistance to cold, heat, fatigue,
Or anything, apparently, but me.
Fine! Say we never see them. I'm already
Half resigned. Half fuming also. These

315

Two halves, a look exchanged, now choose their weapons—
Notebook and cigarette—then step outside
To settle their affair beneath the trees.

The trees! Tall domed communicating chambers,
A dark flight above ground. One duellist
Writes blind: *my piano nobile.* The other
Levels his lighter, fires into the air,
Panicking the nearest green room where
Starlings by now have joined—safety in numbers—
Forces against the Owl. A twittering dither
Fills no less the wisdom-threatened mind . . .
The starlings, though, seem rather to rewind
Our day of human speech, erasing it
At treble speed from the highstrung cassette.
If one could do as much— A last drag. Wrong
To be so—so— Saved by the dinner gong.
I run to dip my hands in water first.
How pale they turn, how innocent, immersed.

2

Umberto's meal: a tablespoon of wine
Stirred into his minestra. While we cope
With eggs and spinach, fruit and cheese, he talks.
The life inside him's like a local clay
Gritty with names, Montale, Berenson,
Edith Wharton making our eyes flash
—Mario's too, who waits in his white jacket.
Plates gleam dimly from the walls' high gloom.
Our host's gaze lidded, voice a purr,
Out comes the story long heard *of.* I wash
It down tonight a shade too greedily—
Hence this impression in blurred chalk:
The famous story of Umberto's walk.

When Italy surrendered to the Allies
In 1943, September 3rd,

The proclamation was five days deferred
Until their main force landed at Salerno.
It was imperative that liaison
Be made with them, in those five days, by (word
Meaning to me anything but certain) "certain
Anti-fascist groups." And as there were no
Lines of communication safe from the Germans,
"Withdrawn," but smelling Naples' every rat,
Umberto offered to get through alone.
The train he boarded, one warm dusk in Rome,
Left after midnight, crept an hour down
The unlit coast; sniffed peril, backed away;
Returned its passengers to Rome at dawn.

Next . . . a bus? a jeep? a peasant's cart?
The vehicle evaporates. Our friend
(To be imagined half a lifetime spryer,
Credentials drily folded to his heart,
Correct as now in city clothes—
Whatever garment, that surreal year,
Betrayed its wearer like an epithet,
Skewfoot, fleet of spirit, dressed in whose very
Visibility to glide unseen
Across a poppied or a blackened field,
A bullet- or a fullmoon-pitted square)
Kept haltingly advancing. Hillsides rang
With the cicada of one sunny parasang.

The social fabric and his place in it
Were such that he knew people everywhere—
People the war had sent like snails
Into their shells, to feed on books and air.
So the stale biscuit and tea-tainted water
Served by a scholar's maiden aunt or sister
Brought him, through a last long stretch of dark,
Face to face with—tree-tall in lamplight—
"A type of Roman hero, your Mark Clark,

Bronze

Beside whom on the Prefettura balcony,
His forces having landed overnight,
I megaphoned next morning—as my one
And only 'moment' on a balcony—
The terms of peace, translated, to the crowd."

"You were the hero," David murmurs, wowed.

3
Now Florence? But a stratagem
We only later analyze—
Bared shoulder and come-hither shrug
Of hill, the spread of golden thighs—
Lures our rented Fiat bug
Away from Them.

And soon enough, to two ecstatic
Oh's, on the horizon shines
Then vanishes, then shines again,
One of those metaphysical lines
Blue-penciled through the pilgrim's brain—
The Adriatic.

Our spirit-level, salt of life!
(Unpack the picnic here?) Above
Lie field and vineyard, castle built
To nurture intellect, art, love
Together with, let's face it, guilt,
Deception, strife.

Below, in brilliant aquarelle,
Undulating dullness fans
Itself to tatters. Bubble-streamers
Betray the scuba-superman's
Downward bent or Jungian dreamer's
Diving bell.

Here at my desk, but fathoms deep,
I've known the veer and shock of schools,
The kiss of inky Mafiosi;
Perusing stanzas like tide pools,
Have seen the stranger flex a rosy
Mussel heap,

And shaken myself clear. The break
Of glib, quicksilver levity,
The plunge of leaden look or phrase
Thudding to rest where none can see . . .
I name just two of the world's ways
Picked by mistake.

Sheathed in a petrifying mitt,
A hand took mine on the sea floor.
That detour (we'll reach Florence yet)
Had to be structural before
Heroes tomorrow stripped of threat
Could rise from it.

4
—Not a moment, poor babies, too soon!
For the Mediterranean will in
Another few decades have perished,
And with it those human equivalents,
Memory, instinct, whatever
In you the first water so joyously
Answered to. These you have fed
To your desktop computers—e basta.
Yes, hard on the heels of God's death,
As reported in Nietzschean decibels,
Follows (writes Mary McCarthy
In Birds of America) *one*
Far more ominous bulletin: Nature
Is dead, or soon will be. And we
Are well out of it, who in the tempest—

Bronze

Exultantly baring through coppery
Lips the carnivorous silver—
Knew best how to throw around weight
And go overboard. Thus we arrived
At the couch of the green-bearded ancient
To suffer the centuries' limpet
Accretions unwelcome as love
From a weakling, cold lessons imparted
Through waves of revulsion, yet taken
How deeply to heart! From their oozy
Sublime we have risen. Dissolving
The clay at our core, sonar probe and
Restorative poultice have brought
The high finish in which we began
Back to light. Your nostalgia completes the
Illusion with flickering tripods,
Where feasters, fastidious stucco
Pilasters, and vistas of shimmering
Water red roses rope off
Make us objects of art. We dislike it
As women in your day dislike
Being sexual objects, but were not
Consulted. To fictive environments
Blood is the fee. And this light,
This pink gel we peer out through (not gods
Like the hurler of levin in Athens,
Not tea-gowned ephebes like the driver
At Delphi, but men in their prime
With the endocrine clout so rebarbative
To the eternally boyish
Of whichever sex) is the shadow of
Light we once lived by, dealt death in,
Dividing the spoils. And it burns
But to spangle the gulf that expires
Between you—still crusted with appetite,
Armed to the teeth by your pitiful
Wish not to harm—and ourselves

Whose much-touted terribilità
Is at last this articulate shell
Of a vacuum roughly man-sized. We
Should rather be silent. Rhetorical
Postures, the hot line direct
To the Kremlin or out of Hart Crane,
Leave us cold. It's for you to defuse them.
For us, in our Dämmerung swarming
With gawkers, what trials of mettle
Remain?—short of meltdown your fantasies
Trigger, then grandly shrug off
With a sangfroid our poor old heroics
Were child's play beside. Go. Expect no
Epiphany such as the torso
In Paris provided for Rilke. Quit
Dreaming of change. It is happening
Whether you like it or not,
So get on with your lives. We have done.

5
Let's do. From the entropy of Florence, dead
Ends, wrong turns, *I told you so*'s, through rings
First torpid then vertiginous, our route
Leads outward into the bright spin of things.
Our separate routes. A month. A year.
Time for Umberto, hobbling under plane
Trees now, now cypressed-in by memory,
To take a last step, crumple, disappear.
Time for Fair David to regain
A small adobe fortress where, beset
By rodent insurrections, howl and hoot,
He turns his skylit oils to the wall rain
Exorbitantly gutters. Time for me,

Who off and on had idolized these two,
To heed a sympathetic twinge.
The doctor probes and listens. Powers failing?

A shot of hormone? The syringe he fills,
At tip one shining droplet, pure foreplay,
Sinks into muscle. And on the third day
Desire floods the old red studio.
A figure reincarnate, wings outspread,
Full quiver, eager lips, from years ago—
My Eros to the life—awaits unveiling.
Friends, here is salvation! Are you blind?
Here, *under* the dumb layers which unwind
I somehow cannot. Tanglingly opaque,
They're nothing if not me. The hidden god,
Unknelt-to, feels himself to be a fake,

The poorest jerky newsreel of dead forces
Breast-deep in waves, that strained for shore,
Bayonets flashing, helmeted young faces
Mad to provoke from the interior
Those attitudes assumed in love and war—
All fair, till peace limps forward on a cane.
The Axis fell. Its partners rose again.
Up came from vaults, for light to kiss awake,
The groggy treasures of the Glyptothek.
Out came war babies. Only the lost life
Held back, reduced to skeletal belief,
Coils of shot film, run-down DNA.
Earth saw to it as usual, clay to clay.

6

All fair? Precisely what, fair friend, umpteen
Stanzas your distance tinges haven't been.
You whom night strips to armature, whom day
Equips with tones to brush desire away,
Painting as much of sheer Experience
(Your holy mountain, that sea-born, immense
Magnet, its fatalities untold)
As one tall window facing north can hold,

Raptly, repeatedly have scaled it, if
Only to canvas. Metamorphs of cliff,
Quarry and timberline, you understand,
Haunt me, too. Come then, "because they're there,"
On with our stories. Make the telling fair.
But first, in all but liaison—this hand.

7

Off the record, but as everyone
Perfectly knew, Umberto was the son
Of his father's friend the King, whose name he bore.
A discreet match, the death of the young bride,
This phantom parentage on either side . . .
Rumor? Yet the King's bust, I recall,
Kept reigning, on its trophied pedestal,
Head and shoulders over a salon
Never in use (gilt horrors, plush, veneer),
The single, token room to have been done
Up for the Contessa. Her demise
Preserved in prelapsarian Empire
And Biedermeier the enchanting rest:
Stained glass and goat-foot chair, blue willows peeling
From gesso'd wall, tent-stripes or clouds from ceiling.

Blows that set our braver products clanging
Level categorically these hanging-
By-a-thread gardens of the West.
Umberto first intended the estate
As a "retreat for scholars." His last will
Left it intact to Mario the butler,
So long devoted and his brood so great.
The house sighed. It had entertained the subtler
Forms of discourse and behavior. Still,
There'd be the baby's tantrum, the wife's laugh,
The old man's groan. New blood. How else redeem
Spells of such cast and temper as to seem
Largely the stuff of their own cenotaph?

8

For in the odd hour made even
Odder as it dawns,
I too exist in bronze.
We were up on the deck, drinking
With summer friends, when Fred
Asked who the bust was of.
Year-round sentinel
On the domestic ramparts,
Acquiring pointlessness
As things we live with do,
It gave me a look back:
The famous, cold, unblinking
Me at six, I said—
Then drifted from his side
To stand by it. Ah yes.

Slowly the patina
Coarsened, paled—no perch
For owl or nightingale.
The local braggart gull
Flaps off and up, its shriek
Leaving a forelock white.
Where the time's flown I wonder.
A deeply-bored eye sees,
Or doesn't, the high trees
Waving in vain for sundry
Old games like Hide and Seek
Or Statues to be played,
Come evening, in their shade.

Losses of the foundry!
As chilling aftermath
Laszlo—my sculptor—made
Headlines one morning: QUEENS
MAN AXED BY SONS. Had they
Also posed for him,
Two trustful little boys. . . ?

Smoothing their brows, the maker's
Hypnotic fingertips
(I still feel my scalp crawl)
Were helpless to forestall
The molten, grown-up scenes
Ahead, when ire and yearning,
Most potent of alloys
Within us, came to grips.

Here Augie, seeing me absent,
Ambled up to rest
Tanned forearms easily
On my unruffled hair.
A tilted beer, a streak
Staining bluegreen my cheek—
Bless him, he couldn't care
Less for the Work of Art!
The stubborn child-face pressed,
Lips parted, to the heart
Under his torn T-shirt
Telling the world *Clean Air*
Or Else, was help and hurt
As much as I could bear.

CHANNEL 13

It came down to this: that merely naming the creatures
            Spelt their doom.
Three quick moves translated camelopard, dik-dik, and
            Ostrich from
Grassland to circus to Roman floor mosaic to
            TV room.

Here self-excusing voices attended (and music,
            Also canned)
The lark's aerobatics, the great white shark's blue shadow
            Making sand
Crawl fleshwise. Our ultimate "breakthrough" lenses took it
            In unmanned.

Now the vast shine of appearances shrinks to a tiny
            Sun, the screen
Goes black. Anaconda, tree toad, alpaca, clown-face
            Capuchin—
Launched at hour's end in the snug electronic ark of
            What has been.

THE BLUE GROTTO

for Mona Van Duyn

The boatman rowed into
That often-sung impasse.
Each visitor foreknew
A floor of lilting glass,
A vault of rock, lit blue.

But here we faced the fact.
As misty expectations
Dispersed, and wavelets thwacked
In something like impatience,
The point was to react.

Alas for characteristics!
Diane fingered the water.
Don tested the acoustics
With a paragraph from Pater.
Jon shut his eyes—these mystics—

Thinking his mantra. Jack
Came out with a one-liner,
While claustrophobiac
Janet fought off a minor
Anxiety attack.

Then from our gnarled (his name?)
Boatman (Gennaro!) burst
Some local, vocal gem
Ten times a day rehearsed.
It put us all to shame:

The astute sob, the kiss
Blown in sheer routine
Unselfconsciousness
Before one left the scene . . .
Years passed, and I wrote this.

RADIOMETER

At sunrise on a pin
Upright within a globe
No bigger than your frontal lobe
Four little blades of tin begin to spin.

One side of each is white
And one side black—
White knowing only to fend off,
Black only to drink in, drink in the light

At first with circumspection, then be hurled
Backwards by noon at dizzying speed
Through the revolving door that gives onto the world;

While forward, just as helplessly,
Ghost-faces hurtle—Yang and Yin?
Phlegm and fervor? You/me?

World without end?
Not this one. Look: the setting sun, my friend.

TREES LISTENING TO BACH

Overture. A shutter opens. Down
Goes light. The Norfolk Island pine
Potted in peatmoss breathes
Deeply once; resigns itself on cue.
Under the dimming dervish crown
Extend now four, no, five fringed limbs
(Twelve more hang downward barely skirting trance)
In stills—in stills that—yes! inspired
Revolve and quicken. As though fingers flew,
Each organ point's plump quiver
Already stitching, radiance
Turning to raiment and back, forth steps a spine
Threadbare in seams picked out by the moonrise.

Wonders who'll itemize? Why, the jade tree,
Budding collector grown
Roundshouldered from its decade in the shade,
A shut-in life. Though short on fun,
It takes note, missing none.
Some nine score pitch-pure, stone-smooth lobes
Store the Courante, the Sarabande's grave strobes.
Exact dynamics are its law,
And juicy, time-consuming pedantry
Its lesson. Fluke or flaw,
Dust in a groove, temptation to emote
And blot performance leaving it unswayed,
Its roc's claw grips a base that creeps clockwise.

Not so two chestnuts in the streetlamp's glow
Champing, manes tossing. No
Obstacle brooked: RUSH to developer
These multiple exposures, bring the sheaf,
Or by now trunkful, up to date
As if their whole belief

Trees Listening to Bach

Racing each night a green crosscountry inch
Depended on it. Time—do they suspect?—
Is changing signature and only stable
These random moments ridden, then reined in,
As now, foam-petal-flecked,
Splattering triplets . . . Here the Gigue dismounts.
The stillness reaches "to the skies".

On the used plate a wash of silver dries.

AFTER THE BALL

Clasping her magic
Changemaking taffeta
(Old rose to young spinach
And back) I'd taken

Such steps in dream logic
That the Turnstile at Greenwich
Chimed with laughter—
My subway token.

SANTORINI: STOPPING THE LEAK

Five sessions of God willing lethal x
Rays on a live target purple-inked
For isolation, and the plantar wart
(Girt by its young, one throbbing multiplex
Neither knife nor acid could abort)
Active half my adult life's extinct
—Whereupon, sporting a survivor's grin,
I've come by baby jet to Santorin.

Inches overhead, a blue that burns,
That all but blackens—heaven as a flue?—
Against this white that all but calcifies.
Behind, a breakneck mile of hairpin turns,
The Golden Climb—mule dung and reek, whips, flies—
Lurches and jolts. Each moment someone new
Arrives at this despaired-of-from-below
Village unmelted on the crest like snow.

A gentler view, south from my balcony:
Past cubes and domes the baked vine terraces
Descend to beaches' black volcanic sand
And pewter glare of the September sea.
Mechanically a pencil guides my hand,
Then bells ajangle through the diocese
Bring the next balcony to life. Who's there?
Nelláki toweling her short silver hair.

She's not been idle, not our girl. It seems
We come provided with an introduction
To three old maiden sisters here, who set
A table that exceeds her wildest dreams
Of gourmandise. The ladies must be met,
And to that end I fear she's taken action:
Dispatched a note. A day or two should bring
Their summons. Meanwhile, homework, sightseeing!

The reason I've not made this trip before
Is that it would be—is—magnificent.
One wanted the companion who might
Act on a hushed injunction, less to ignore
The worst than stroll through it by evening light,
Made into courtyards (whitewashed, some for rent)
Where even stone-deaf Nelly hears her name
Spoken by mute bursts of nasturtium-flame.

Which color added, I've prepared my palette—
White, silver, black, night purple, dab of lake
For cliff-coagulations that regress
To null mist at a blow from the moon mallet.
Brushes? These five of mine with nothingness
Threatening forever to unmake
The living form it sees through in a trice—
A challenge to hold steady, these suffice.

Innermost chaos understood at first
As Gaia's long-pent-up emotions crippling
Her sun-thrilled body, spun to the great Lyre;
Pent up, but all too soon unleashed—outburst
Savage enough to bury in its fire
The pendant charms she wore, palace and stripling,
A molten afterbirth transmuting these
Till Oedipus became Empedocles—

Leaper headlong into that primal scene
And deafening tirade. The mother tongue
At which his blood boiled, his brain kindled. Ash
Of afterthought where once the sage had been,
Louse in a log . . . Or else, supposing flesh
Withstood temptation, could a soul that clung
To its own fusing senses crawl at last
Away unshriveled by the holocaust?

Santorini: Stopping the Leak

The curtain on a universal hiss
Would fall; steam cover all; millennia pass.
An island surface. Two. Three. Vineyards wax.
The plume of smoke with airier emphasis
Slant from the inky crater. Paperbacks
About Atlantis map the looking-glass
Rim of that old disaster, deep salt blue
Unrippling oval noon sun peers into.

Apart from the volcano and the wine,
The place, I read, was famous for its vampires.
People we inquire of shrug and stare—
No matter. Clearly, as the gods decline,
An eerie radiation fills the air
And eats their armor. The Byzantine Empire's
Avian-angelic iridescence
Shrank to black flitterings in the lymph of peasants.

Nelly agrees, but wears a child's gold cross
One hadn't seen, and wants to start with snails
Smothered in garlic. She's put in her hearing
Aid—we can talk. Out of the blue the loss,
Young, of her twin brother flickers, searing
Us both an instant; then her gaze drops. Veils
Of sheer belated comprehension blur
This little tumbler lifted, drunk to her.

Dear soul. Maria called her La Petite.
She has a modesty of scale and scope,
No use for buried motives, double vision:
Not one, beyond the voltage that a sweet
Dessert infuses, or a street musician,
To draw the lightning. Yet her isotope
Perished forever in it. As the waiter
Brings fresh wine, the grim, drowned point breaks water.

Not that I've lost or am about to lose
More than on the one hand (or one foot)
An ingrown guest, and on the other, well,
Greece itself. Corrupted whites and blues,
Taverns torn down for banks, the personnel
Grown fat and mulish, marbles clogged with soot . . .
Things just aren't what they were—no more am I,
No more is Nelly. The good word's goodbye

—Or so at least the radiologist's
Black box thought, humming it for all prognosis.
Goodbye. One smelt it as a scorching, read
The heat in shielded eyes and sausage wrists
Throughout his waiting room, where each was fed
Terror and time in exact, equal doses.
As for our meal tonight—which far-out lab
Prepares and serves it: Gemini? the Crab?

We must be light, light-footed, light of soul,
Quick to let go, to tighten by a notch
The broad, star-studded belt Earth wears to feel
Hungers less mortal for a vanished whole.
Light-headed at the last? Our lives unreal
Except as jeweled self-windings, a deathwatch
Of heartless rhetoric I punctuate,
Spitting the damson pit onto the plate?

And if (weeks later, Athens) life still weighs
Too heavily, why, leave the bulk behind.
Give M the bed. Let what was done in it
Parch at a glance from certain killing rays,
And the trunk-oubliette's black yawn admit
Such pictures, records, books as we've consigned,
Poor well-bred things in panic, to the freighter
(Bound for yet more life) Prestidigitator.

Santorini: Stopping the Leak

On this last evening, once tiny flames
Have danced within my pupils to consume
Letters and photographs, once M, dead drunk,
Muttering of bad faith, though he "names no names",
Has sobered up enough to lift the trunk,
Alone I've stretched out in a rifled room,
Aching for sleep. There comes to me instead
—Brilliantly awake but cased in lead—

A cinéma-mensonge. Long, flowing fits
Of seeing—whose? Utterly not my own:
Bayonet fixed, one olive-skinned Iraqi
Guarding the stairwell of a wartime Ritz;
The look outflashing from his brass and khaki,
That single living cell needed to clone
In depth a double, phantom yet complete
With skills and jokes, cradle to winding-sheet;

His moonbaked slum, muezzin cry and tank
Rumble, the day Grandfather plucked the goose,
The sore in bloom on a pistachio-eyed
Tea-shop girl above the riverbank
—Vignettes as through a jeweler's loupe descried,
Swifter now, churning down the optic sluice,
Faces young, old, to rend the maître d's
Red cord, all random, ravenous images

Avid for inwardness, and none but driven
To gain, like the triumphant sperm, a table
Set for one—wineglass, napkin, and rosebud?
Or failing that, surrender to blue heaven
Its droplet of pure ego, salt as blood?
The warm spate bears me on, helpless, unable
Either to sink or swim, though knowing whence
My trouble springs. Psychic incontinence.

A ghost-leak in the footsole. Fighting free
Of sheets that flap off spectral over tiles,
Like bats in negative, sobbing for air
I hobble to the mirror, wordlessly
Frame this petition to its oval, where
Behind a twitching human curtain smiles
Those revels' Queen, in easy ownership,
Sated, my vigor coloring her lip:

I whose demotic commune at your kiss
Took on new senses, snowflake-singular
Facets and symmetries, even as I fall
Back out of mind, yours, anyone's to this
Upsteaming human thaw, babble and brawl
Of now no thought, O that the shattered star,
The music-maker, broadcast limb from limb,
Be made whole, Lady—hear and remember him!

No answer. Or—? In gloom the peevish buzz
Of a wee wingèd one-watt presence short-
Circuiting compulsively the panes
Gone white. *My* drained self doesn't yet . . . yet does!
From some remotest galaxy in the veins
A faint, familiar pulse begins. The wart,
Alive and ticking, that I'd thought destroyed.
No lasting cure? No foothold on the void?

Its tiny secret agent watchful still,
Just where I'd counted on—say an oblivion
That knew its limits. Here was Santorini
Once more, blue deeps, white domes, in imbecile
Symbiosis with the molten genie.
I hear the ferrous, feather-light diluvian
Lava clink at a knife-tap from our guide;
Once more attain, Nelláki at my side—

Santorini: Stopping the Leak

Grumpy all day because a civil note
Had come by hand, before the morning mail,
Professing the three sisters "desolate"
(One with lumbago, one with a sore throat,
The third with friends in Athens—well, that's Fate)
Not to receive us. So goodbye, roast quail,
French wines and pastries briefer than a bubble . . .
We must be light!—once more attain the double

Site of our last excursion: Prophet Elias'
Radar-crowned monastery, reached by mule.
(Oven, winepress, lentil boutique, and loom.
A sunken door. We rose from hand and knee as
Oil lamps awoke an underground classroom.
Here, throughout centuries of Turkish rule,
Small pupils widening, their abbot set
Before them bread and wine—the Alphabet

Pruned of meaning to dry glottal kernel,
Gaunt root and stock that, quickened, resurrect
Sibyl and scribe's illuminated leaves—
Food for thought even now in this nocturnal
Limbo of straw children, scarecrow sleeves
Lifting their Book of Life mute with neglect,
While overhead a flickering in fetters
Descended on the office of dead letters.)

Behind us then. Next, down and up the gorge,
To gain, past a toy chapel to Saint Michael,
The precinct of Apollo of the Herds
—Of tourists? Not that day. A heavenly forge,
Hammer and tongs, our solitude, our words
Snapped up by North Wind, bellowed to recycle
The bare, thyme-tousled world we'd stumbled on,
Its highbrow wholly given to the Sun

Who beamingly returned the gift. We felt
A stone heart quicken, a deep fault made whole.
Far and wide round us infant waters laughed.
But He meant business also. Having knelt
In amused piety, and photographed
Our Friend, *and* fingered, open-mouthed, the hole
Burnt through my film—by one split-second glance!—
I drew a breath. So much for radiance.

Here, finally, music that would take Satie
Twenty-five hundred years to reinvent
Put naked immaturity through paces
Of a grave dance—as if catastrophe
Could long be lulled by slim waists and shy faces.
Our "worst" in part lived through, part imminent,
We made on sore feet, and by then *were* made,
For a black beach, a tavern in the shade.

A NOTE ABOUT THE AUTHOR

James Merrill was born in New York City on March 3, 1926, and lived in Stonington, Connecticut. He was the author of twelve books of poems, which won him two National Book Awards (for *Nights and Days* and *Mirabell*), the Bollingen Prize in Poetry (for *Braving the Elements*), the Pulitzer Prize (for *Divine Comedies*) and the first Bobbitt National Prize for Poetry awarded by the Library of Congress (for *The Inner Room*, 1988). *The Changing Light at Sandover* appeared in 1982 and included the long narrative poem begun with "The Book of Ephraim" (from *Divine Comedies*), plus *Mirabell: Books of Number* and *Scripts for the Pageant* in their entirety; it received the National Book Critics Circle Award in poetry for 1983. *Late Settings* appeared in 1985. In addition to the one volume edition of his narrative poem *The Changing Light at Sandover,* he also issued two selected volumes: *From the First Nine, Poems (1946–1976)* (1982), and *Selected Poems 1946–1985* (1992). He was the author of two novels, *The (Diblos) Notebook* (1965, reissued in 1994), and *The Seraglio* (1957, reissued in 1987) and two plays, *The Immortal Husband* (first produced in 1955 and published in *Playbook* the following year), and, in one act, *The Bait*, published in *Artist's Theater* (1960). A book of essays, *Recitative*, appeared in 1986, and in 1993 a memoir, *A Different Person*. His last book of poems, *A Scattering of Salts*, was published in 1995, following his untimely death on February 6 of that year.

A NOTE ON THE TYPE

The text of this book is set in a film version of Plantin, the design of which is based upon one of the types acquired by the firm of Christopher Plantin of Antwerp after his death. Originally a Frenchman, Plantin was born at Saint Avertin, near Tours, about 1520. He settled eventually in Antwerp and began his printing business in 1555, establishing a type foundry in connection with the press in 1563. His work made Antwerp a great center of printing, but it should be noted that he depended almost entirely on the French for his types; among his suppliers were Robert Granjon and Claude Garamond. The present typeface named in his honor is a free adaptation originally issued by the Monotype Corporation in 1913.

Printed and bound by Fairfield Graphics, Fairfield, Pennsylvania

Designed by Harry Ford